KEY STAGE 3

• KEY STAGES IN HISTORY •

MEDIEVAL REALMS

R J Cootes

Nelson

Thomas Nelson and Sons Ltd
Nelson House Mayfield Road
Walton-on-Thames Surrey
KT12 5PL UK

51 York Place
Edinburgh
EH1 3JD UK

Thomas Nelson (Hong Kong) Ltd
Toppan Building 10/F
22A Westlands Road
Quarry Bay Hong Kong

Thomas Nelson Australia
102 Dodds Street
South Melbourne
Victoria 3205 Australia

Nelson Canada
1120 Birchmount Road
Scarborough Ontario
MIK 5G4 Canada

First published by Thomas Nelson and Sons Ltd 1992

ISBN 0-17-435057-0
NPN 9 8 7 6 5 4 3 2 1

Printed in Hong Kong.

Acknowledgements
The author and publishers are grateful to the following for permission to reproduce copyright material:

AA Picture Library: pages 67, 75, 79;
Aerofilms: page 28 *(above)*;
J Allan Cash: pages 83 *(above)*, 110;
Ancient Art and Architecture Collection: pages 16, 19, 34, 44, 54, 56, 100;
Board of Trustees of the Royal Armouries: pages 10, 107 *(below)*;
Bodleian Library, Oxford: pages 23, 32 (Trinity College Cambridge), 47;
Bridgeman Art Library: pages 30 *(above)*, 31 (Louvre, Paris), 48 (British Library) *(bottom right)*, 60 *(bottom left)*, page 86, 108 (Fine Art Society);
British Library: pages 33, 39 *(below)*, 40, 43, 44, 48, *(centre and bottom left)*, 51, 84, 92 *(above)*, 93, 97, 101;
A & C Black: pages 45, 89;
Cambridge University Collection: pages 17 *(above)*, 18, 30 *(below)*, 37, 70, 71;
Amanda Clarke: page 12;
Conway Library: page 27;
Corpus Christi College Cambridge: page 60 *(above)*;
Dean and Chapter of Westminster: pages 61, 62, 69, 73 *(left)*, 94, 95;
e.t. archive: pages 28 *(below)*, 50 (Honourable Society of the Inner Temple), 103 *(above)*;
Fitzwilliam College, Cambridge: page 41;
Clive Hicks: page 24;
Hulton-Deutsch Collection: pages 91, 106
Sonia Halliday Photographs: page 63;
Michael Holford: pages 7, 8, 9 *(above)*, 14, 17 *(below)*, 35, 58, 81 *(below)*, 102;
Michael Jenner: pages 53, 76;
A F Kersting: pages 26, 42, 83 *(below)*;
Mansell Collection: pages 29, 59, 80, 90 103 *(below)*, 104, 105;
Master and Fellows of Christ Church College, Oxford: page 75;
Museum of London: page 10;
National Museum of Wales: page 72;
National Library of Scotland: page 73 *(right)*;
National Portrait Gallery: page 107 *(above)*;
Public Record Office, London: pages 22, 48 *(top left)*, 49;
Royal Museum and Art Gallery, Canterbury: page 78;
Rex Features: page 85 (PH Brooker);
Science Museum: page 87 *(bottom right)*;
Science Photo Library: page 9 (Barney McGrath);
Shuel: page 109;
Trinity College Cambridge: page 39 *(above)*, 92 *(below)*;
Trustees of the British Museum: page 81 *(above)*;
Windsor Castle Library: page 65 (© 1991 Her Majesty the Queen).

If any credit has been inadvertently omitted, we will be pleased to rectify this at the earliest opportunity.

Preface

To make this book both interesting and accessible to eleven- and twelve-year olds, great care has been taken to use clear, straightforward language. To allow adequate scope for explaining ideas and concepts, the basic text has been given a more generous allocation of space than is commonly found at this level. Experience of young readers suggests that extreme brevity rarely aids understanding or stimulates enduring interest.

The selection of material has been determined by the relevant core study unit of the National Curriculum. Most of the prescribed topics have been incorporated into chapters with a chronological structure. This allows for the integration of social and economic with political history and gives the reader a framework for developing some sense of time. For ease of reference, all the topics in the Orders are highlighted in bold type in the *Index*.

Sources – both written and pictorial – are numbered consecutively in each chapter. Not all are keyed into the text, to make the book easier to read. There are textual references to all written sources, but only to those picture sources which directly support the narrative. All documentary extracts are provided with brief introductions to set them in context and have been carefully edited and glossed; they have not been paraphrased because this would destroy their 'period flavour'.

The *Assessment Tasks* at the end of each chapter cover all three Attainment Targets in a structured and balanced way, taking account of the double weighting of AT1. The additional groups of questions in the body of the text are designed to stimulate both general discussion and clarification of historical terms and references. Many are also relevant to the Statements of Attainment.

I should like to thank my wife, Sarah, and my collaborator, L.E. Snellgrove, for their encouragement, help and advice.

Richard Cootes.

To the reader

Meaning of the terms 'medieval' and 'Middle Ages'

Those who study history – called historians – find it useful to divide the past into large 'periods' of time. You will already have come across such terms as *ancient times* or the *Ancient World*, referring to the oldest period of human history. At the other end of the scale, historians call the most recent period of history – roughly the last 500 years – *modern times* or the *Modern Age*.

The years in between ancient and modern history are called *medieval times* or the *Middle Ages*. The Latin words for Middle Age are *medium aevum*, and this is where the word medieval comes from. Obviously men and women living at that time did not think of themselves as 'medieval people'! Each person's own lifetime is, to them, the latest age. All such periods of history were invented long afterwards by historians who saw some shape or pattern in the past.

Contents

1 From Duke to King

The Norman Conquest

On the morning of 28 September 1066 hundreds of ships appeared off the south coast of England, near Pevensey in Sussex. Surprised onlookers would first have seen mastheads and sails all along the horizon. As the fleet drew closer, they would have heard on the wind the excited shouts of soldiers, the clanking of their weapons and the neighing of horses. England was about to be invaded by an army of six or seven thousand men led by William, Duke of Normandy.

How did the Norman invasion of 1066 come about? Much of this chapter and the next are concerned with its causes and consequences. We are able to piece the story together from *chronicles* (histories) written by people living at the time. You will be able to read parts of these sources for yourself, translated from the original Latin or Old English. For example, **Source 1** is about William's army crossing the Channel.

The story of the invasion is also told in a famous piece of needlework called the Bayeux tapestry. Like a cartoon strip, it shows men sailing the seas (**Source 2**), building castles, feasting, fighting and dying. It was embroidered in eight colours of wool on pieces of linen sewn together in a strip 70 metres long and half a metre wide. The tapestry was probably made by English women, soon after 1066, at the orders of William's half-brother, Bishop Odo of Bayeux. Today it is preserved behind a glass frame in a special exhibition gallery at Bayeux, where thousands of people flock to see it every year.

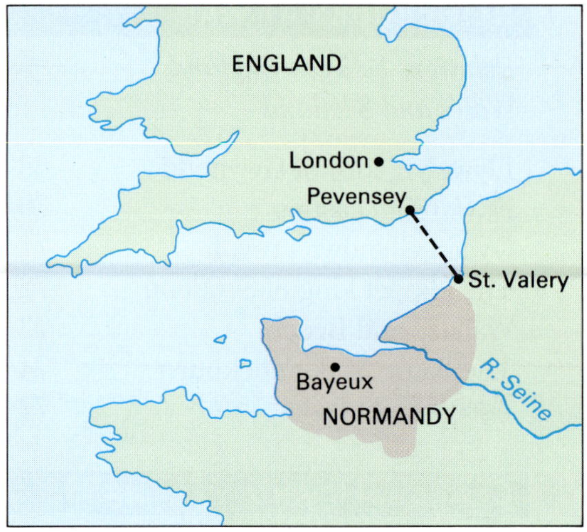

The position of Normandy.

SOURCE 1

This was written about seven years after the Norman invasion, by William of Poitiers, one of Duke William's personal priests.

When at last the longed-for wind blew, prayers were offered to Heaven and … all rushed to board the ships, their only fear being that they might be left on the shore. The Duke himself, hot with excitement, bellowed orders to anyone he thought was lagging behind … During the night the ships got underway … There were so many that they looked like a forest of trees bearing sails … They were driven by a favourable wind to Pevensey where they landed unopposed.

William and Harold: rivals for the Crown

William invaded England claiming to be its rightful king. He knew that a leading English nobleman, Harold Godwin, had been made king only nine months earlier. But William said Harold should not have accepted the Crown because it had already been promised to him. What were the rights and wrongs of this quarrel?

The English king before Harold, Edward 'the Confessor', had no children.

SOURCE 2

Part of the Bayeux tapestry, showing William's invasion fleet at sea. What does this tell you about the Norman ships – especially the way they were driven and steered?

When he died, in January 1066, the only remaining Englishman of royal blood was his nephew's small son, Edgar. But the nobles and Church leaders who made up the king's council (known as the Witan) decided Edgar was too young to rule. These were dangerous times and the English needed a strong king without delay.

Nowadays there are laws to decide who will be king or queen. When a ruler dies the Crown passes automatically to the next in succession. But 900 years ago there were no fixed rules. Often the Crown went to the man the previous king chose to follow him. We are told that this happened in 1066: King Edward, on his deathbed, named Harold Godwin, Earl of Wessex, as

WHO WERE THE NORMANS?

- The Normans, or 'Northmen', were descendants of Vikings – pirates who sailed from the lands we now call Scandinavia.
- While some vikings were settling in the British Isles, the Normans gained control of part of northern France (AD 911). This became Normandy.
- These tough, seafaring folk were soon influenced by the French people around them. They were converted to Christianity and learned the French language.
- The Normans also copied French methods of warfare. They used knights on horseback and built castles with moats and defensive walls.

WHO WERE THE ENGLISH?

- The English, or Anglo-Saxons, came from the continent of Europe and began settling in Britain in the fifth century. They soon became Christians.
- They were later joined by viking invaders. For a time England was ruled by viking kings – Cnut and his sons (1016–42).
- England's rich soil is good for farming, which helps to explain why it was often invaded by its European neighbours.
- English methods of warfare had changed little over the centuries. Unlike the Normans, the English all fought on foot.

SOURCE 3

The following comes from the *Anglo-Saxon Chronicle*, a history of England up to 1154 written by monks.

> After the burial [of King Edward] the underking Harold, earl Godwin's son, whom the king before his death had appointed successor to the kingdom, was elected to the throne by the nobles of the whole realm. On the same day he was crowned and blessed by Aldred, archbishop of York.

SOURCE 4

This comes from a *Life of King Edward*, written very soon after his death. The author is unknown, but is thought to have been a visitor from the Continent who spent time at Edward's court.

> When King Edward returned from France [in 1041] quite a number of men of that nation, from important families, came with him ... He enriched them with many honours and they became his close advisers and organised the royal palace ... Consequently he offended many of the nobles of his kingdom ... And as a result his realm gradually became disturbed.

his successor (**Source 3**). Harold was the most powerful man in England and the commander of Edward's army. No one doubted his courage and skill as a soldier. The Witan lost no time in confirming him as king.

William flew into a rage when he heard the news. He claimed that Edward had promised the Crown to *him* some years before. This was probably true. Edward had grown up in Normandy under the care of William's father. He had many Norman friends and advisers in his household (**Source 4**). In 1051, according to the *Anglo-Saxon Chronicle*,

> Duke William came from overseas with a large following of Normans, and King Edward and his companions treated him honourably and sent him back to Normandy with many rich gifts.

It is likely that Edward's promise was made at this time. Perhaps he failed to keep it because he thought that the English nobles would not accept a Norman as king.

According to William, not only Edward but Harold too had promised to help him get the Crown! Norman chroniclers tell us that this happened in 1064. Moreover the Bayeux tapestry shows Harold going to Normandy and taking a sacred oath to obey and serve William (**Source 5**). We do not know whether Harold took the oath willingly. William may well have put pressure on him. If he did, Harold would not have been obliged to keep his word. William, however, was in no doubt. He declared Harold an oath-breaker (**Source 6**) and prepared for war.

SOURCE 5

The Latin words on this part of the Bayeux tapestry say: 'Where Harold made an oath to Duke William'. We see Harold standing with one hand on an altar and the other on a chest containing holy *relics* (remains) of saints.

SOURCE 6

In the Christian Church, the breaking of an oath was considered a very serious sin. This was the view of William of Jumièges, a Norman monk writing in about 1070.

Without delay, Harold unjustly took his (Edward's) kingdom, breaking the oath which he had sworn to the Duke. The Duke at once sent messengers who pleaded with him to withdraw from this madness and keep the faith which he had sworn. He not only refused to listen but caused the whole English people to be faithless to the Duke.

SOURCE 7

The Bayeux tapestry shows the appearance of a comet with a fiery tail (see top border). The people pointing to it seem frightened. On the right, an astrologer tells King Harold that the comet is a sign of misfortune to come. Why do you think there are ghostly outlines of ships in the bottom border?

Victory at Stamford Bridge

In the spring of 1066 a comet appeared in the sky and shone brightly for a week. Modern scientists call it Halley's comet. We now know that it appears at regular intervals, roughly every 76 years. But the English people living in 1066 believed it was a sign from God warning them of some future disaster (**Source 7**).

During the summer Harold assembled an army on the south coast and stationed his fleet nearby. Meanwhile, across the Channel, William's men built ships and gathered supplies. By August, William was ready, but he was stopped from sailing because the wind was in the wrong direction. Harold, too, was ready to fight in August. When the invasion was delayed, things began to go wrong for him. It was harvest time and many of his soldiers wanted to go home. By early September, with food stocks running low, Harold had to disband his army and also send his ships to London for fresh supplies. The Channel was left undefended.

QUESTIONS

1 Why do you think Harold is referred to as the 'underking' in Source 3?

2 Can you explain why Edward's conduct would have offended the English nobles (Source 4)? How might this have affected their attitude later, when William claimed to be Edward's successor?

3 Which side would you expect the author of Source 4 to have been on in 1066? Give reasons for your answer.

4 Why do you think Source 3 does not mention Harold's oath to William and Source 6 does not mention the Witan's choice of Harold as king?

SOURCE 8

Halley's comet, (Left), photographed on its most recent appearance, in 1986. It is named after Edmund Halley who, in 1704, was the first to calculate its orbit and demonstrate that it reappears at regular intervals.

SOURCE 9

The *Anglo-Saxon Chronicle* describes the battle of Stamford Bridge.

Harold our king came upon the Norwegians by surprise ... and that day a very hard battle was fought by both sides. Harald Hardrada and earl Tostig were killed and the remaining Norwegians made to run away, while the English fiercely attacked them from the rear until some reached their ships ... The King then spared the life of Olaf, the son of the Norwegian king ... and all those who were left aboard the ships. They then went ashore to our King and swore oaths that they would remain ever peaceful and friendly.

Harold now received dreadful news. The much feared King of Norway, Harald Hardrada, had landed a large army on the north-east coast of England. The same north wind that kept William's ships in port assisted Hardrada's voyage from his base in the Orkney Islands. With him was Harold Godwin's brother, Tostig – a traitor to his country. Tostig had been banished from his earldom in England the previous year and now hoped to win back his lands with Hardrada's help. Hardrada's aim was to conquer England and win the Crown.

The invaders won a battle near York on 20 September against two powerful northern earls, Edwin and Morcar. By then the English King was already on his way north, gathering an army as he went. Hardrada and Tostig seem to have been taken by surprise when the English attacked them, on 25 September, at Stamford Bridge near York. Both were killed in the fighting and their forces were crushed (**Source 9**).

Harold did not have long to celebrate his victory. Messengers soon arrived to tell him that William had landed in Sussex. The wind had been a good friend to William. It had kept him in Normandy when the English King was ready to do battle and, instead, brought Hardrada's attack in the north. Now it allowed William to land while Harold was far from the scene.

Harold marches south

Harold quickly covered the 190 miles back to London with his bodyguard of trained soldiers, called *housecarls*. He probably

SOURCE 10

The main weapon of Harold's *housecarls* was the viking battle-axe. It was fixed to a handle about a metre long and swung with both hands. It could knock off a man's head with one blow.

SOURCE 11

English *housecarls* and Norman knights protected their bodies with chain-mail shirts similar to the one pictured here. Chain-mail was made out of hundreds of small metal rings joined together and sewn on to a backing of leather or strong linen.

had well over a thousand of these tough warriors, carrying huge battle-axes and shields. The rest of the English army consisted of ordinary farmers and tradesmen. Some had axes or spears; others probably nothing more than farm implements such as scythes. These men were recruited by their county sheriff for up to 40 days' military service a year. Not many who fought against Hardrada would have made the long journey south. Harold called for fresh recruits from the southern counties to face the Normans.

William, meanwhile, moved his army a few miles along the coast to Hastings, where he built a castle of timber. His soldiers were generally better armed and equipped than Harold's. About a third of them were knights who fought on horseback with lances and shields. He also had archers who could fire arrows up to 150 metres. Other Norman footsoldiers are shown in the Bayeux tapestry armed with swords or spears and carrying shields. Many on William's side were not Normans at all. They had come from other parts of France, encouraged by promises of lands in England if William won.

Harold stayed only a few days in London, gathering reinforcements, before heading for Sussex. He could probably have had many more soldiers if he had waited for them to arrive from the surrounding counties (**Source 12**). On the other hand, reports of destruction by the Norman army must have made Harold anxious to defend his kingdom as quickly as possible.

In the end Harold probably had six or seven thousand men – much the same as William. Nine miles from Hastings, Harold halted and camped for the night on a hill where the village of Battle now stands. He was almost certainly expecting extra forces to join him. William seems to have realised this. Rather than wait for the English strength to increase, he moved his army inland and attacked the English position in the morning.

SOURCE 12

The *Anglo-Saxon Chronicle* describes events leading up to the battle of Hastings.

The King (Harold) marched his army towards London with all speed; and although he knew very well that many of the better warriors in all England had fallen in the two battles [against Hardrada] and that half his army had not yet come in, he nevertheless did not hesitate to meet his enemy in Sussex as quickly as he could. Nine miles from Hastings he gave them battle, before a third of his army was drawn up.

1066: movements of the rival armies.

The battle of Hastings

The fighting began at about 0930 on Saturday 14 October. First, William's archers showered arrows on the English ranks. This his knights galloped up the slope and tried to scatter the opposition. But the English kept in close formation behind a 'shield wall' (**Source 14**). After several hours of fierce fighting the result was still in doubt. Then, we are told, William ordered his knights to pretend to retreat (**Source 15**). This tempted many of Harold's men to break ranks and chase after them. The Normans turned on their attackers and cut them down.

Gaps now appeared in the wall of English shields. As the evening shadows lengthened, the Normans finally broke

SOURCE 14

In the centre of this scene from the Bayeux tapestry we see Harold's *housecarls* forming a wall of shields to resist the attacks of the Norman knights. Among them is a single bowman. This reminds us that the English army contained only a few archers.

SOURCE 13

A view of the battlefield from the Normans' position. The English wall of shields stretched all along the ridge at the top, with King Harold in the centre – where the abbey now stands.

SOURCE 15

Here is part of an account of the battle of Hastings written by the Norman priest, William of Poitiers. Although he was not present at the battle, he would have known a number of eyewitnesses, including Duke William himself.

The English were greatly helped by the advantage of the high ground, which they could defend by … their great numbers massed together and their weapons which could easily find a way through shields … The Normans and their allies, realising they could not overcome an enemy so great in numbers and standing so firm without great loss to themselves, retreated, deliberately pretending to run away … Some thousands [of English] boldly launched themselves as if on wings after those they thought to be running away. The Normans, suddenly wheeling their horses about, cut them off, surrounded them, and killed them on all sides, leaving not one alive. Twice they used the same plan with the same effect…

William … was a noble general, turning back retreat, inspiring courage, sharing danger … Three horses were killed under him. Three times he leapt to his feet, unalarmed, and took swift revenge…

As the day wore on the English army realised beyond doubt that they could no longer stand against the Normans. They knew that they were reduced by heavy losses and that the King himself … had fallen … They therefore retreated and made off as soon as they got the chance, some on stolen horses, many on foot.

QUESTIONS

1. Taking an army with horses across the sea in small wooden ships was a very risky thing to do. Can you think of ways in which it could have ended in disaster for William?
2. In Sources 9 and 12, what is the attitude of the *Anglo-Saxon Chronicle* towards Harold?
3. What does Source 14 tell you about the way in which soldiers on both sides were armed?
4. If the high ground the English occupied was a great advantage (Source 15), why did William seem so keen to begin the battle?

through. Harold was killed, (**Source 16**) along with two of his brothers and many of his noblemen. Right to the end, he was brave and tireless in defending his kingdom. As darkness fell, the remains of the English army fled. One of the most important battles in European history was over.

The throne was vacant but William was not yet master of England. He marched to London by a roundabout route (see map), forcing the surrender of important towns on the way. The only serious English resistance came at London Bridge. Rather than fight on a narrow wooden bridge, William decided to encircle London and approach from the north. To discourage opposition, he burned and destroyed the countryside on the way. At Berkhamsted a group of leading Englishmen, including the northern earls Edwin and Morcar, met the Duke and accepted him as king. He was crowned William I on Christmas Day 1066 in Westminster Abbey.

Timeline

1042–66	Reign of Edward 'the Confessor'
1051	Duke William's visit to Edward
probably 1064	Harold's oath to William
1066	6 January – Harold crowned April – Halley's comet 25 September – battle of Stamford Bridge 14 October – battle of Hastings 25 December – William crowned

Assessment tasks

A *Knowledge and understanding*

1 Of all the possible reasons for the Norman invasion of England, which do you think was the most important, and why?

2 Here are six possible causes of the English defeat at the battle of Hastings. Add more if you wish.

- William took Harold by surprise.
- Normans used mounted knights in battle; the English all fought on foot.
- The north wind stopped William from sailing when Harold was ready for him.
- Many of William's soldiers were volunteers who stood to gain personally from a victory.
- The Norman army was better armed and equipped.
- Many of the English were tired after the long journey to fight Harald Hardrada.

Place these in what you consider to be their order of importance. Give reasons for your answer.

SOURCE 16

The death of King Harold as shown in the Bayeux tapestry. The words above say: 'King Harold is killed'. Historians still argue about whether he is the man with the arrow in his eye or the one being struck down by a Norman knight.

3 Luck seems to have played an important part in the events of 1066. Can you think of at least *three* occasions when William appears to have been lucky or Harold unlucky?

B *Interpretations and sources*

4 Here are two accounts of Harold's succession to the English throne written by twentieth-century historians.

> Harold virtually seized the throne. On the very day that Edward was being buried at his new church and abbey at Westminster, Harold had himself proclaimed by a Witan composed only of his friends and allies ... He had little solid foundation upon which to build his claim to the loyalty of Englishmen ... He could count upon a following only in the south ... The rest of the island was either lukewarm or hostile to him.
> (Edwin Tetlow, 1974)

> In the eyes of the English, the successor to the throne was obvious, for at home Harold's claims were quite undisputed ... Edward had on his death-bed named him as his heir ... and for twelve years Harold had been the real protector and ruler of the kingdom ... [He] obtained the consent of a witan [containing] such members as happened to be in the neighbourhood of London at the moment ... The claims of William of Normandy were not considered ... Not an English voice was raised on William's behalf in January 1066 and not an English hand was lifted to help him when he landed in the country in the following September.
> (G.O.Sayles, 1948)

a On what points do these accounts disagree?
b Are the disagreements based on fact or opinion, or both?
c Which of the two accounts do you find most convincing, and why?

5 **a** For what purpose do you think the Bayeux tapestry was made?
b How does your answer to (a) affect its value as an historical source?

6 Look again at the account of the battle of Hastings written by William of Poitiers (Source 15).

a If you did not know that the writer was on the Norman side, how would you be able to tell from this passage?
b William of Poitiers was inclined to exaggerate. Can you find any likely examples in Source 15?
c How far is this account of the battle backed up by the picture sources in the chapter?

2 The rule of the Conqueror

Norman England

Many English nobles had died in the great battles of 1066 or fled overseas. King William gave their lands to barons he had promised to reward for fighting for him. 'The Conqueror', as he was later called, allowed Englishmen to keep their lands if they swore to support him. But he did not trust them. During his frequent stays in Normandy – where he still ruled as duke – William left England in charge of Norman lords.

The Conquest completed

The English were harshly treated by their foreign masters. Soldiers stole and damaged property. Cruel and unjust acts often went unpunished. Houses in many towns were knocked down, and families made homeless, to clear the way for castle-building. Not surprisingly, the King and his barons soon faced rebellions in several parts of the kingdom.

The most serious threat to William came in 1069. Thousands of northern English joined up with a viking army from Denmark and captured York. Although outnumbered, William won a crushing victory and scattered the rebels. To prevent further trouble the King took a terrible revenge. He led his men through northern England and burned the countryside, destroying everything in sight (**Source 2**).

William faced one last rebel stronghold, at Ely in the flat, marshy lands of East Anglia. The leader of the rebels was an English noble, Hereward 'the Wake' – so-called because he was wide awake and watchful. When William attacked, in 1071, he needed boats to get his army across the marshes. But although he killed most of the rebels, Hereward escaped. Many stories are told about Hereward's adventures, but no one knows for sure what happened to him. It had taken William five years of hard fighting before he could really call himself master of England.

SOURCE 1

William I, as shown on a silver penny from his reign

SOURCE 2

King William's revenge after the 1069 rebellion was called 'the Harrying of the North' (to harry is to destroy or lay waste). It is described here by Orderic Vitalis, a monk who was half English and half Norman. He was writing about 50 years after the rebellion.

William ... made no effort to control his fury and punished the innocent with the guilty. In his anger he commanded that all corn and cattle, goods and food of every kind should be gathered up and burnt to ashes, so that the whole region north of the [river] Humber might be stripped of all means of nourishment. As a result ... so terrible a famine fell upon the humble and defenceless people that more than 100,000 Christian folk of both sexes, young and old alike, died of hunger.

Norman castles

William's barons built castles to defend themselves against rebellion. There was no time to lose, so the earliest castles were made of wood rather than stone. Where possible, they were built on high ground. But if the land was flat a large mound of earth, called a *motte*, was made, leaving a deep ditch all round (**Source 3**). This provided the base for a tower, or *keep*, which was surrounded by a wooden fence .

The keep was usually occupied only when the castle was being attacked (**Source 4**). The castle's living quarters,

SOURCE 3

The earthworks of this twelfth-century motte and bailey castle can still be clearly seen at Pleshey, near Chelmsford in Essex. The ditch surrounding the castle was filled with water, making it a *moat*. The bridge between the motte and bailey was built of bricks in about 1400, replacing earlier wooden structures.

SOURCE 4

In this scene from the early part of the Bayeux tapestry, Norman knights are attacking a motte and bailey castle at Dinan in France. On the right, the keys of the town are being offered to Duke William on the end of a lance as the garrison surrenders.

storage huts and stables were built beside the motte in the *bailey* – a courtyard enclosed by a fence, bank and ditch. In time, these 'motte and bailey' castles were strengthened. Stone walls replaced fences around the keep. The result was a *shell-keep* – a wooden tower protected by a hard outer ring or 'shell' of stone (**Source 5**).

To capture such castles, attackers brought up ladders or wooden *siege towers* which were tall enough for men on top to shoot arrows into the keep. They also tried to make holes in the walls by firing boulders from machines like catapults or using tree-trunks tipped with iron as battering-rams. In defence, the castle-guards fired showers of arrows, dropped boulders from the walls and tried to set fire to ladders or siege towers. If attackers failed to break into a castle they might camp nearby and try to starve out the defenders by cutting off their food supplies.

No baron could build a castle without the King's permission. William wanted to be sure that castles were only in the hands of his most trusted supporters. Some were given the task of building and guarding royal castles to control the main towns. In

QUESTIONS

1. What was the point of building castles on high ground?
2. Find the motte in Source 4 and describe what has been built on top of it.
3. In Source 4, by what method are the attackers trying to destroy the castle? Why would it often have been effective in this period?
4. Can you explain why the main entrance of a castle was usually on the first floor, up a flight of steps?

SOURCE 5

The remains of a Norman *shell-keep* still overlook the town of Launceston in Cornwall.

towns such as London and Colchester, William built stone keeps or 'great towers', usually square in shape (**Source 6**). These were by far the strongest Norman castles; many more were built under William's successors.

Stone keeps were dark, draughty places to live in. But they were built for safety rather than comfort. They usually had three or four floors inside. At ground level, food and weapons were stored. The main entrance was usually on the first floor, reached by a flight of steps outside and protected by a *portcullis* – a strong, spiked door which could be raised and lowered. This led into a great hall, the main room of the castle where meals were served. The walls of stone keeps were too high for siege towers to reach and too thick for catapults and battering-rams. Usually the best method of attack was to try to starve out the guards.

SOURCE 6

The White Tower – built (1078–90) to guard the approach to London up the river Thames. Nearly 30 metres high, with walls up to 5 metres thick, it replaced an earlier wooden castle put up by William. Other buildings have been added since the Conqueror's day, making up what we call the Tower of London.

Feudal lordship

In return for their lands, Norman barons had to fight for the king whenever he needed them. At the same time they had to provide knights on horseback; the exact number depended on the size and value of their lands. The need to give military service in return for land is known as *feudalism* or the *feudal system* (the Latin word *feudum* means property held from a lord).

William kept about a quarter of the kingdom for himself. On these royal estates he and his companions hunted the deer, fox and wild boar. The remaining land was shared out among the nobles – barons, bishops and abbots of the larger monasteries. These were the king's *tenants-in-chief*. Before each received his estates he performed a ceremony of *homage*. He knelt, placed his hands between the king's and said: 'I promise to become your man, to hold these lands faithfully and perform my due service'. Then the king told him he must always be ready to fight for him and bring a certain number of knights; it might be five or as many as fifty (**Source 7**).

SOURCE 7

Bishops and abbots provided knights for the king but did not have to go to war themselves. In this document, from 1072, an abbot is told to make sure the King's army assembles in his district.

William, king of the English, to Aethelwig, abbot of Evesham, greeting. I order you to summon all those who are under your supervision that they should bring before me at Clarendon on the Octave of Pentecost [the eighth Sunday after Whit] all the knights they owe me, properly equipped. You, also, on that day shall come to me, and bring with you fully equipped those five knights which you owe me in return for your abbey.

In areas where rebellion was likely, barons often kept their knights close by, living in their castle. But usually a tenant-in-chief divided up some of his lands and gave his knights small estates, or manors, of their own. In this way knights became *under-tenants* and were able to support themselves. An under-tenant swore homage to his lord, just as the tenant-in-chief had done to the king.

William could call on at least 5000 knights altogether. To keep up this fighting strength, new recruits had to be trained. A boy began to prepare for knighthood at about the age of seven, serving as a page in a lord's household. At around fifteen he became a knight's *squire*, or personal servant. A squire learned to ride, wear armour and use weapons so that he could go with his master into battle. When he reached manhood he was ready to be a knight himself. In a ceremony in front of his lord, a sword and spurs were fastened on and he swore to be brave and loyal.

Ordinary peasants played a very important part in the feudal system. They had the right to farm strips of land on the manor and, in return, worked for part of the week on their lord's own estates, called the *demesne* (pronounced demain). This was not very different from the way most country folk had lived before 1066. Instead of holding their land from an English nobleman, most peasants now served a French-speaking lord of the manor.

THE 'FEUDAL SYSTEM' – land held in return for services

William I as shown in the Bayeux tapestry

THE KING

The 'feudal lord' or owner of the kingdom.

Keeps about a quarter of all the land as *royal estates*. Divides the rest among his tenants-in-chief

TENANTS-IN-CHIEF

Mainly barons & bishops
[About 200–300]

Tenants-in-chief promise to obey the king and support him in war, mainly through the services of their under-tenants.

They keep some estates, or *manors*, and divide the rest among their under-tenants

UNDER-TENANTS

Mainly knights
[About 5000]

Under-tenants promise to be loyal to the king and their lord, and support both by their service, usually in war.

They keep some land, or *demesne*, and divide the rest among their peasants

PEASANTS

Village labourers
[About 1½ million]

Peasants support their lord by working on his demesne farm for a certain number of days each week.

They support their own families by farming their strips of land on the manor

Domesday Book

In the last years of his reign William faced many enemies. He fought his rivals in France and had to defend England against threats of invasion by Scots, Welsh and Danes. As well as his feudal knights, William recruited many extra soldiers in Normandy. These were paid mainly out of taxes on his English subjects. The King wanted to be sure that he was getting all he could from taxation. So at the end of 1085 he ordered a detailed survey of England to be made without delay. He wanted to know all about his tenants' lands and the taxes he could expect from them (**Source 8**).

The kingdom was divided into seven areas and each visited by a team of royal investigators. These were trusted men, usually of high rank. They had to check the King's existing records of manors and find out whether the taxes got from each could be increased. So at the local courts in each shire they questioned witnesses, from barons to ordinary villagers. For each manor, they asked who was the lord, who had held the land before 1066, what the land was worth and how much of it was ploughland, meadow, pasture and woodland. They also wrote down details of the villagers and the number of watermills, fishponds and livestock (**Sources 9 and 10**).

The survey was finished before the end of 1086. William would not have had much time to study the results as he was about to leave for Normandy. The records for most of England were re-written in a shortened form and later bound in a large book known as Great Domesday. Detailed returns from the counties of Norfolk, Suffolk and Essex seem to have been left in their original form. These are bound in a second volume known as Little Domesday.

Domesday means the Day of Judgement. The book got this name because the facts in it could not be ignored or avoided by anyone, just like the Judgement Day. Its pages show very clearly the tremendous upheaval brought about by the Norman Conquest. Across the kingdom English nobles had been replaced by foreigners. Out of 180 tenants-in-chief holding the richest estates, only two were English. Nearly all high-ranking people at that time were men, but a few women do appear in Domesday Book. For instance Judith, Countess of Northumbria and Huntingdon, held large estates – including manors given by her uncle, the King.

SOURCE 8

The Anglo-Saxon Chronicle, still kept by the monks of Peterborough, tells us of important discussions the king had with his tenants-in-chief at Christmas 1085. (A *hide* was a piece of land large enough to support a household.)

The king had much thought and very deep discussion with his council about this country – how it was settled and with what sort of people. Then he sent his men over all England, into every shire, and had them find out how many hundred hides there were in the shire, what land and cattle the king himself had in the country, and what taxes he ought to have each year … He had it investigated so strictly that there was not a single hide nor a yard of land, nor indeed (it is shameful to tell but it seemed no shame to him to do) one ox nor one cow nor one pig left out.

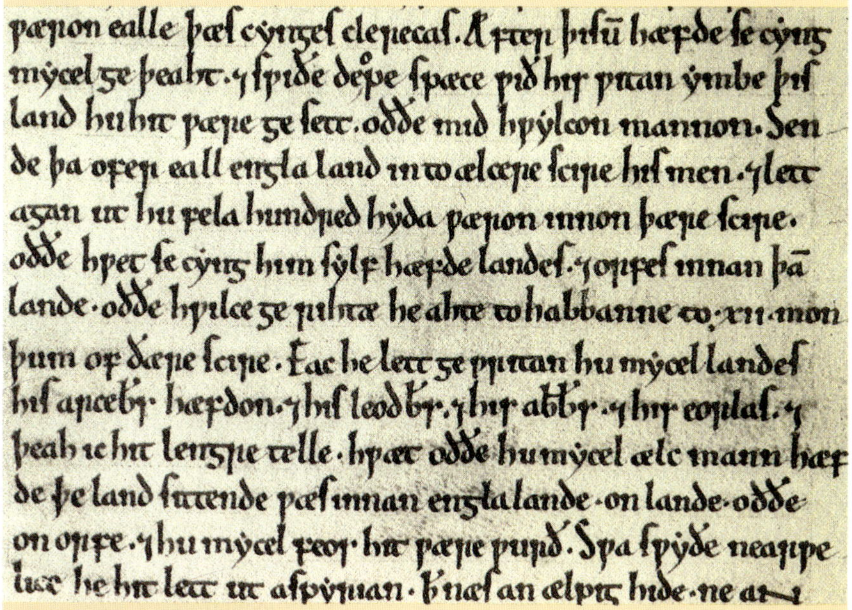
wæron ealle þæs cynges clerecas. Æfter þisū hæfde se cyng
mycel geþeaht. 7 swiðe deope spæce wið his witan ymbe þis
land hu hit wære gesett. oððe mid hwylcon mannon. Sen
de þa ofer eall Englaland into ælcere scire his men. 7 lett
agan ut hu fela hundred hyda wæron innon þære scire.
oððe hwet se cyng him sylf hæfde landes. 7 orfes innan þā
lande. oððe hwilce gerihta he ahte to habbanne to .xii. mon
þum of ðære scire. Eac he lett gewritan hu mycel landes
his arcebis. hæfdon. 7 his leodbis. 7 his abb. 7 his eorlas. 7
þeah ic hit lengre telle. hwæt oððe hu mycel ælc mann hæf
de þe land sittende wæs innan Englalande. on lande. oððe
on orfe. 7 hu mycel feos hit wære wurð. Swa swyðe nearwe
he hit lett ut aspyrian. Þ næs an ælpig hide ne an

Source 8 looks like this – in an early twelfth-century version of the *Anglo-Saxon Chronicle*. In the second line you can see the words *deope spaece*, meaning deep speech or discussion.

SOURCES 9 and 10

These extracts from Domesday Book show that Birmingham and Leeds, now great cities, were tiny villages in 1086.

Richard holds Birmingham of *William*. There are 4 *hides*. There is land for 6 ploughs; there is one plough in the *demesne*. There are 5 *villeins* and 4 *bordars* and 2 ploughs. There is a wood half a mile long and 4 *furlongs* broad. In the time of Kind Edward it was worth 20 shillings, and it is still worth the same. In King Edward's time *Ulwine* held it.

A Norman under-tenant

A hide was a piece of land large enough to support a household

Unfree peasants or villagers who farmed strips of land on the manor

A furlong or 'furrow–long' was about an eighth of a mile, or the length of the average furrow in a ploughed field

William fitz Ansculf, a tenant-in-chief of the King

Land Richard kept for himself

The English *thane*, or lord, of Birmingham before 1066

Peasants with less land than villeins. Those with even less than bordars were called *cottars* (cottagers)

In Leeds there are 10 *carucates* and 6 *bovates* of land for *geld*. There is land for 6 ploughs. *T.R.E. 7 thanes* held it for 7 manors. Now there are 27 villeins there and 4 *socmen* and 4 bordars have 14 ploughs. A priest is there, and a church, and a mill worth 4 shillings a year and 10 *acres* of meadow. It *was* worth 6 pounds: now 7 pounds.

Tax paid to the King

Danish equivalent of a hide; the land a plough team (usually eight oxen) could keep cultivated. Taxes were based on the number of carucates

These English (or Anglo-Saxon) nobles normally had at least 5 hides of land and a house. Richer ones had grand halls

One bovate was equal to an eighth of a carucate

Socmen or *sokemen* were free holders of land. They often owed rent or services to the lord of the manor, but were free to leave (and in some cases sell) their land

In the time of King Edward (in Latin, *Tempore Regis Edwardi*)

An acre was a day's ploughing for a team of oxen. It later became a standard measurement

Before 1066 (or in the time of King Edward)

SOURCE 11

The two volumes of Domesday Book (the open one is 'Great Domesday'). They are listed as Document Number 1 at the Public Record Office, London.

The Conqueror's sons

William I met his death in the summer of 1087 while fighting against the King of France. In the town of Mantes his horse took fright and threw him heavily on to the iron *pommel* (knob) on the front of his saddle. The sixty-year old King was seriously injured and died a month later (9 September). His admirers remembered him for his courage, determination and devotion to the Christian Church (**Source 12**). Many others thought him hard, cruel and greedy (**Source 13**).

The Conqueror divided his lands and wealth between his three sons. Henry, the youngest, got 5000 pounds of silver. Robert, the eldest, became Duke of Normandy. The English crown went to William, the second son and his father's favourite. William II was short, stocky and red-faced, which explains his nickname 'Rufus' (Latin for red). Rufus was a strong king; his subjects were afraid to disobey him. But he was also harsh and unpopular. 'In his later years', said the chronicler William of Malmesbury, 'his desire to do good grew cold, and evil ripened within him ... for he feared God but little, man not at all.'

Rufus died when an arrow struck him in the chest while he was hunting in the New Forest (August 1100). His companion, Walter Tirel, admitted firing it but said it was an accident. The King's brother, Henry, was quick to claim the throne – taking advantage of the absence of his elder brother, Robert, on a foreign war. Henry seized the royal treasure in Winchester and had himself crowned in London only three days after Rufus's death. As a man, Henry I was just as cruel as his father and brother before him, and even more hungry for money. But he was a

SOURCES 12 and 13

Here are two different views of William the Conqueror. The first was written in Normandy shortly after his death by a monk in the abbey of Caen. The second is the work of an Englishman, Henry, Archdeacon of Huntingdon, writing early in the next century.

12 The king was wiser than all the rulers of his time ... He was never discouraged from doing anything because of the work involved, and he was never afraid of danger ... If his voice was harsh, what he said was always right for the occasion. He followed the Christian way of life, in which he had been brought up as a child, and whenever his health allowed he regularly and with great reverence attended Christian worship each morning and evening.

13 He was wise, but crafty; rich, yet greedy; glorious, but his ambition was never satisfied. Though humble to those who served God, he was hard and unbending towards those who held out against him ... He squeezed thousands [of pounds] of gold and silver from his most powerful tenants, and burdened his subjects with the labour of building castles for him. If anyone killed a stag or a wild boar, his eyes were put out, and no one dared complain. He cared for beasts of the hunt as if they were his children; so that to create the hunting ground of the New Forest he ordered churches and villages to be destroyed, and, driving out the people, made it a place for deer to live in.

SOURCE 14

King Henry I is shown to the left of the mast in this twelfth-century drawing.

SOURCE 15

William of Malmesbury wrote history books during the reign of Henry I. Here he describes King Henry's concern for justice and fairness. (An *ell* was a measurement of length based on an outstretched arm.)

He ruthlessly hunted down robbers and counterfeiters (forgers), and punished them severely when they were caught … He corrected the false *ell* used by traders by measuring his own arm and making it the standard for all England. He made it a rule for the followers of his court that, no matter which of his estates he was on, they should obey his orders as to what things they should take without payment from the country folk, how much they should purchase and at what price. He punished those who disobeyed with heavy fines or even death.

QUESTIONS

1. Can you give a reason why William I's eldest son only became a duke while his second son became a king?
2. Some think that Henry I plotted the murder of William Rufus. How might he have given cause for suspicion?
3. What is the attitude of the writer of Source 15 towards Henry I?
4. Lords and peasants carried on speaking different languages in England for about 300 years. Why do you think this went on for so long?

SOURCE 16

Like many old churches in England, this one – in Melbourne, Derbyshire – still contains Norman stonework: rounded arches and windows, thick walls and massive pillars.

firm, wise ruler who tried to make all his subjects obey the law (**Source 15**).

England went through many changes under William I and his sons. The Norman Conquest brought with it new ideas of feudalism and led to widespread castle-building. It resulted in the rebuilding of many churches, cathedrals and abbeys (see Chapter 3). It also brought a new language – Norman French. In time, many French words found their way into the English still spoken by ordinary peasants. The link with Normandy led to more trade and travel across the Channel. In future years England gained from having closer contact with the rest of Europe.

Assessment tasks

A *Knowledge and understanding*

1 What were the main consequences of the Norman conquest of England? Divide up your answers into two groups, as follows:
- **a** short-term consequences – those which affected people immediately;
- **b** long-term consequences – those which affected people over many years, or in the future.

2
- **a** Why did the Normans build castles?
- **b** When the Romans invaded Britain, 1,000 years earlier, they built forts. What were the main differences between Norman castles and Roman forts?

3 Write down any *three* important changes to life in England that occurred under William I or his sons. Did these make life better or worse for ordinary people? Give reasons for your answers.

B *Interpretations and sources*

4 Two modern historians have this to say about the death of William Rufus.

> It is impossible to avoid altogether the suspicion that Rufus's death was the result of a conspiracy in which his younger brother and successor was involved. Henry was present at the hunting expedition. As soon as he heard of his brother's death, without waiting to see the body removed for burial, he turned his horse's head and galloped to Winchester, to secure the royal treasure ... The speed of Henry's seizure of the throne ... [raises the question] whether he could have been crowned in Westminster three days after his brother died in Hampshire if there had been no preparation.
> (Christopher Brooke, 1963)

> We are completely in the dark. That Henry should seize the opportunity to take the crown does not mean that he was privy to (aware of), or had engineered, a plot. Hunting accidents were common. [Tales of conspiracy], although entertaining, are usually pure fiction.
> (Frank Barlow, 1955)

- **a** In what ways are these accounts (i) similar, and (ii) different? Can you suggest a reason for the difference?
- **b** Why do you think there is such disagreement about Rufus's death?

5
- **a** Are the writers of Sources 2, 8, 12 and 13 for or against William I?
- **b** Using these sources and other information in Chapters 1 and 2, write your own character study of William.

6 What can you say about Birmingham and Leeds from the information given in Domesday Book (Sources 9 and 10)? For example, can you estimate their size and population (and compare these with present figures)?

3 A Purpose in Life
The Medieval Church

It is hard for us to understand how much religion meant to medieval people. All around they saw suffering and grief, as lives were cut short by disease, war and brutality. This made them think about death a lot. They looked for a meaning and purpose in life, and found it in religion. The Christian Church taught that death led to eternal happiness for those who followed the ways of Christ. It also taught that sinners would burn for ever in the fires of hell.

People were reminded of the Christian faith throughout their daily lives. Most fine buildings were religious; so were nearly all books, pictures and ornaments. On Sundays everyone rested from work and went to church. They did the same on a number of other 'holy days' in the year (this is how we get the word holiday). Hardly anyone would have understood the Latin words of the church services. But the strangeness of the language probably made things seem all the more impressive.

SOURCE 1

Wall-paintings in churches often showed imaginary scenes of Heaven and Hell. This is part of the Last Judgment from the village of Wenhaston in Suffolk. The damned are being herded into the Mouth of Hell – in the form of a huge sea-monster.

The Church of Christendom

Nowadays there are many different kinds of Christians, such as Church of England, Catholics, Quakers or Methodists. However in medieval times the Christian religion was the same for all. In the British Isles and nearly all of Europe, there was just one, Catholic (which means universal) Church, headed by the Pope in Rome. The Christian countries of Europe were together known as Christendom.

In every Christian country wealthy people hoped to save their souls by making gifts to the Church. These often took the form of land on which to build churches. So over the centuries the Church of Rome became immensely rich and the largest landowner in Europe. It collected its own taxes, made its own laws and had its own law-courts. As head of this great Church, the Pope was a powerful figure, able to influence kings and princes.

The Norman Conquest linked England with Normandy and so brought it closer to the rest of Christendom. It also led to the replacement of leading English churchmen with Normans. By 1080 only one of the kingdom's sixteen bishops was an Englishman. Under Norman rule, cathedrals and abbeys built before 1066 were demolished and replaced by Norman-style buildings. At the same time hundreds of new parish churches were built in England.

SOURCE 2

The medieval parish church at Hanwell in Oxfordshire. Churches were usually a lot larger than they needed to be, because they were built to glorify God as well as make room for the parishioners. This one has had many bits added on over the years. For example, on the right of the picture, where the roof changes, a new *chancel* (the part containing the altar) was added. Where else can you see signs of later additions?

Bishops and priests

Before 1066, English bishops usually lived quiet, simple lives. The Normans who replaced them were often rich and powerful, with palaces, large estates and many servants (**Source 3**). We saw in Chapter 2 that bishops were tenants-in-chief of the king. This meant they attended his great council and played a part in governing the country. Most bishops were well–educated and hardworking but often their way of life cut them off from ordinary people.

SOURCE 3

This description of a Norman bishop, Robert Bloet, was written in the early part of the twelfth century by Henry of Huntingdon, himself an archdeacon.

When I was a child, a boy and a young man, I used to see the glory of Robert, our bishop, his gallant knights, his noble pages, his costly horses, his vessels of gold and silver gilt, his store of plate, his gorgeous waiting-men, his purple robes and fine linen, and I thought there could be no happier condition. And … [even though he] loved and valued things of the world too much … Bishop Robert was gentle and humble, helping to advance many and putting no one down, the father of orphans, beloved by his household.

A bishop looked after a large area called a *diocese*. This was divided into parishes, each with a priest. The bishop had to see that his parish priests did their job properly (**Source 5**). He was helped in this task by an archdeacon, who was known as 'the bishop's eye'. Bishops also performed religious ceremonies called sacraments. Among these was *holy orders* – the final step to becoming a priest. No women were allowed to take holy orders, and this is still the rule in the Catholic Church today.

Another law of the Catholic Church which has lasted to our own day forbids its clergymen to marry. Instead of having a family of his own, a priest was expected to give all his time to the needs of his parishioners. He held daily services, visited the sick and taught people about the Bible and the Ten Commandments.

Parish priests got some income by charging fees for baptisms, weddings and burials. In country parishes they also had a share of the farming land, called the *glebe*. All parishioners were expected to give a *tithe* (tenth) of everything they produced to the priest, for the benefit of the Church (**Source 6**). Most of this went to the bishop, but some would be kept in the parish to help the poor, sick and elderly.

SOURCE 4

The cathedral at York. A bishop's church was called a cathedral because it contained his *cathedra* (throne). Cathedrals were usually built in the shape of a cross, with the short arms, or *transepts*, facing north and south. The main body of the church, the *nave*, lies to the west. The remaining part, called the *choir*, extends eastwards to the altar.

SOURCE 5

When a bishop or archdeacon made a 'visitation' to inspect a parish, ordinary parishioners called sidesmen were questioned about various things, including the priest's behaviour. The following comes from the record of a visitation, in 1301, to a parish near Exeter in Devon.

St Mary Church The parishioners say that … the Vicar feeds his beasts of all kinds in the churchyard, by whom it is evilly trodden down and vilely fouled … he causes his malt to be malted (beer to be brewed) in the church, where he stores his wheat and other goods; so that his servants go in and out and leave the door open, and the wind blowing into the church at time of storms is liable to uncover the roof. They say moreover that he preaches well … when he is present. But he often departs to live at Moreton-Hampstead [on Dartmoor] for a week or a fortnight, so that they have then no priest.

SOURCE 6

This fifteenth-century woodcut shows peasants paying their *tithes* to the priest. One is leading a lamb, another is carrying a goose. Country folk paid tithes in animals or crops. In the towns, craftsmen and traders usually paid a tenth of the value of the goods they made or sold.

The monastic life

Some early Christians believed that the best way of leading a holy life was to give up their belongings and live in a remote cave or hut, away from the temptations of the world. These were the first monks. The word monk means 'one who lives alone'. Later, however, monks gathered in small communities to work and pray together.

In the sixth century an Italian monk, Benedict of Nursia, wrote a *Rule* for such communities to live by. This 'Benedictine Rule' – which is in fact a large number of rules – is still practised today in many countries. It requires monks to make three basic *vows* (promises to God). These are poverty, which means giving up money and goods; chastity, which forbids sexual relationships; and obedience,which means keeping the rules of the community and obeying the abbot in charge (**Source 7**).

The daily life of a medieval monastery began before dawn and was strictly timetabled. Eight times a day everyone gathered in the church or chapel to sing and pray to God. In between, many hours were spent on manual labour (work with the hands) such as farming or building. Women who took up the religious life (called nuns) usually did lighter work such as spinning wool or needlework. But they made the same vows as monks and worshipped in similar ways.

For hundreds of years Benedictine communities set an example of good Christian living. But by the time of the Norman Conquest most monasteries in England and on the Continent had become less strict. Beds had got softer, clothing more comfortable and there was usually plenty to eat. Monks did less manual labour and spent more time reading and copying out books.

Early in the twelfth century, in France, several communities of monks returned to the strict, simple ways of Benedict – who had by now been made a saint by the Church. The most successful were the Cistercians, named after their first abbey, at

SOURCE 7

Here are some extracts from the Benedictine *Rule*, written in the early part of the sixth century.

Idleness is an enemy of the soul. Because this is so the brothers ought to be occupied at particular times in manual labour, and at other fixed hours in holy reading ... they are truly monks when they live by the labour of their hands.

No one, without the abbot's permission, shall give, receive or keep as his own anything whatever: neither book nor writing-tablet nor pen ... beds shall be frequently searched by the abbot to guard against the vice of hoarding.

Monks must not grumble about the colour or rough material of their clothes.

A monastery ought to be so arranged that everything necessary – that is, water, a mill, a garden, a bakery – may be made use of ... so that there shall be no need for the monks to wander about outside. For this is not at all good for their souls.

SOURCE 8

Early fifteenth-century painting showing nuns at a service. The reasons for becoming a nun were not always religious. A nunnery offered peace and safety in a violent world. Probably many women who entered nunneries were escaping from an unwelcome or unhappy marriage. Others became nuns because they had no husband and feared being alone.

SOURCE 9

Benedictine monks at a service in their chapel. They were known as 'Black Monks' because of their black robe, or *habit*. The Cistercians were called 'White Monks' from their habits of undyed woollen cloth.

SOURCE 10

One of the great Cistercian abbeys in England was Rievaulx (pronounced Reevo) in Yorkshire, founded in 1132. A Scotsman called Ailred, who later became its abbot, went there in 1134. This is how he described life at Rievaulx.

Our food is scanty, our garments rough; our drink is from the stream and our sleep often upon our book. Under our tired limbs there is but a hard mat; when sleep is sweetest we must rise at a bell's bidding ... There is no room for self-will; no moment for idleness ... Everywhere there is peace, everywhere calmness, and a marvellous freedom from the noise of the world.

SOURCE 11

Ruins of Fountains Abbey, a twelfth- century Cistercian monastery near Ripon in Yorkshire. Most monastic orders kept to much the same layout of buildings.

- Buildings not shown here include barns, stables, workshops, a bakehouse, brewery, water-mill and almonry (where poor people could get free food and clothing)

QUESTIONS

1. St Benedict taught that 'to work is to pray'. Can you explain what he meant by this?
2. Why do you think Fountains Abbey (Source 11) was built on the banks of a river?
3. Can you explain why Fountains Abbey did not have a school?
4. Why did a person require some education to be a monk or nun?

Citeaux. They spread rapidly throughout western Europe, including England. Cistercians built their abbeys in remote areas, far from towns. They ate the plainest food, wore a rough robe of undyed wool and devoted much of their day to manual work, particularly farming.

In England, Cistercians settled mainly in wild and lonely parts of the North (**Source 10**). Here they turned hillsides into sheep pastures and produced great quantities of wool. At first, they lived in rough wooden huts. But with the money they got from selling wool they were able to hire craftsmen to build fine monasteries and churches.

The big Cistercian abbeys were like farming businesses, with many fields of crops and thousands of sheep and cattle. To help with the work, the monks employed *lay brothers*. These men did not have the schooling to be monks, but they made the same vows. Life was hard for lay brothers, yet there was no shortage of willing recruits. To an uneducated peasant, being a Cistercian lay brother promised a secure life on earth and a sure way to heaven.

The friars

Francis Bernardone was the son of a rich merchant from Assisi in Italy. He grew up living in luxury. But in 1207, when he was about twenty-five, he suddenly gave up everything to devote his life to God. He did not, like the monks, shut himself off from the world. Instead he travelled from place to place, preaching the Gospel and helping the poor. Francis refused to have any money or possessions. He begged for food and shelter wherever he went.

St Francis of Assisi, as he is now called, was a kind and gentle man. He loved all living creatures and taught people to love one another. His example of simple, holy living soon attracted a band of followers. They gave up everything they owned to join Francis and become his *friars* (brothers). It was the beginning of a new religious society, or order, called the Franciscans (**Source 13**).

SOURCE 12

St Francis of Assisi preaches to the birds in this famous picture by the Italian painter Giotto (1266/7–1337). Giotto was one of the first medieval artists to make the shape and movement of the human body look natural in paintings.

SOURCE 13

To guide the Franciscan order, a *Rule of St Francis* was written, with the Pope's approval, in 1223. It includes the following.

The brothers shall possess nothing, neither a house, nor a place, nor anything. But ... they shall seek charity with confidence, and not be ashamed, for the Lord made Himself poor in this world for us.

I strictly command all the brothers never to receive coin or money ... Those brothers to whom God has given the ability to work, shall work faithfully and ... as the wages of their labour they may receive bodily necessities for themselves and their brothers but not coin nor money.

All the brothers must be clothed with simple and rough garments, and may repair them with pieces of sackcloth, or with other remnants.

I advise, warn and instruct my brothers ... that when they go into the world they shall not quarrel, nor argue, nor judge others. But let them be gentle, peaceable, modest, merciful and humble.

A second order of friars, the Dominicans, soon appeared – founded by a Spaniard, Dominic de Guzman (later St Dominic). They gave up worldly goods, like the Franciscans, and were also required to have a deep knowledge of Holy Scripture. Many Dominicans were university scholars. When they preached, in towns and along the roadside, they told interesting stories and were often very witty. Before long crowds were flocking to hear them.

SOURCE 14

A monk working in the *Scriptorium* (writing room) of his monastery. Benedictine monasteries in particular were centres of learning and education. Most historical records of the Middle Ages were written by monks. They also saved and copied precious books from the past and so preserved knowledge of ancient civilisations.

A group of Dominicans arrived in England in 1221; the Franciscans followed three years later. Both went to the poorest, dirtiest parts of towns, ignoring the risk of disease. However, as time went by, friars, like the monks before them, found it hard to stay poor and humble. They too were given lands by rich men and built themselves friaries to live in. But whatever their failings in later years (see Chapter 10) the friars stirred up enthusiasm for religion. And by founding schools they did much to advance education.

Teaching and learning

Education in medieval times was controlled by the Church. Teachers were nearly all men who had taken holy orders – priests, monks and friars. And most schools were in monasteries and cathedrals. So close was the link between education and religion that when a man was called a clerk it meant that he was both a churchman and also able to read and write.

Most people never got the chance to learn reading and writing. Some peasants' sons were given lessons by their local priest, but usually they learned just simple Latin to help them follow the church services. Schooling for girls was not even considered in peasant families. However both sons and daughters of well-to-do parents were taught basic Latin and French at home, usually by a priest. After that, boys would often go to serve as pages in a neighbouring household, where their schooling continued.

To get a more advanced education, a boy would first need a thorough knowledge of Latin grammar. Most 'grammar schools' were attached to cathedrals, monasteries and friaries. However, by the fourteenth century they were being founded by wealthy merchants in the towns. Grammar schools were tiny by modern standards, usually with just one teacher and perhaps 20 or 30 boys. The pupils often spent nine or ten hours a day, six days a week, studying Latin. Those who

QUESTIONS

1. Look again at Source 12. Why do you think the artist showed Francis in this way?
2. It was said that the appearance of the friars did much to raise the standards of ordinary priests in the Church. Can you explain why?
3. Children of well-to-do families learned French rather than English (at least until the fourteenth century). What was the reason for this?
4. Can you think of a reason why young people used the margins of books for practising their alphabet (Source 15)?

made good progress might get the chance to learn other subjects, such as arithmetic or geometry.

Books were very expensive because they had to be copied by hand on parchment, made from animal skins (**Source 15**). Usually the teacher had the only copy of the book being studied. He would read aloud, sentence by sentence, and get pupils to write notes or recite until they had learned it by heart. Those who made mistakes were flogged with birch rods.

Despite the dull teaching and frequent beatings, many boys grew to love learning. Some went on to advanced studies in law, medicine and divinity (the study of the Scriptures). Teachers of these subjects gathered in a few towns which became known as centres of learning. This is how the universities of Oxford and Cambridge began, early in the thirteenth century. Students, some as young as fourteen, came from far and wide (**Source 17**).

Medieval scholars were often content to hand on knowledge from the past rather than think for themselves. Few questioned the writings of the ancient Greeks or the founders of the Christian Church. One who did was Roger Bacon (1210–90), an Oxford teacher. He said educated men should investigate the world around them.

SOURCE 15

Richard de Bury, who became Bishop of Durham in 1333, was a collector and lover of books. Here he describes some of the ways in which valuable parchment books were misused by the young.

You will see by chance some wilful youth, sitting lazily at his studies … his finger-nails are filthy, black as jet, and with them he marks the place where the subject-matter takes his fancy … He does not care about eating fruit or cheese over his open book, nor about moving his cup carelessly over it … But especially we must keep away from touching our books those shameless youths who, when they have learned to shape the letters of the alphabet, straightaway … decorate with their monstrous alphabets all broader margins that they can find around the text.

SOURCE 16

A medieval school.

SOURCE 17

University students were often accused of unruly behaviour. These fifteenth-century regulations issued by King's College, Cambridge, show the sorts of things the authorities were trying to stop.

We command … that no scholar … may keep … dogs, hunting or fishing nets, ferrets, falcons or hawks … Furthermore, we forbid … all games which provide an opportunity for gambling money or goods. And it is our will firmly … to prohibit … shooting arrows, or casting or hurling stones, javelins, wood, clods … whereby … the Chapel or Hall or other buildings … may suffer any sort of harm or loss in the glass windows, walls, roofs … or any other part.

Bacon himself built an observatory for studying the stars. But Church leaders accused him of doubting Christian teachings about the universe and put him in prison.

Pilgrims and crusaders

A pilgrim is a person who travels to a place believed to be holy. Such journeys, or pilgrimages, were very popular in the Middle Ages. Some churches had shrines (tombs) containing the bodies of saints. People believed these had special powers, particularly of healing. So those with diseases journeyed to touch a shrine in the hope of being cured. Other pilgrims went to pray for special favours or just to have a good time.

SOURCE 20

A crusader knight. Notice his chain-mail and crusader's cross. Pope Urban II declared that God would forgive the sins of anyone killed while fighting on a crusade.

The most popular place of pilgrimage in England was Canterbury Cathedral. It held the shrine of St Thomas Becket who was brutally murdered there in 1170 (see page 52). On the way to Canterbury and other shrines pilgrims often travelled in groups, for company and as protection against robbers. Some pilgrims went abroad, to the shrines of St Peter and St Paul in Rome or to Compostella in Spain, where St James was thought to be buried. However the greatest pilgrimage of all was to Jerusalem and the Holy Land of Palestine, where Christ lived and died.

To the horror of Christians all over Europe, Jerusalem was captured by Muslim Turks in 1087. Now Christian pilgrims who went there feared for their safety. There were stories of pilgrims being tortured or sold in slave markets. Urged on by the Pope, (**Source 19**) kings and nobles from many countries, including France and England, raised an army to go to free Palestine from the Turks. The soldiers sewed crosses on their clothing. They were known as Crusaders, from the Latin word *crux*, meaning a cross.

The Crusaders won back Jerusalem in 1099 and slaughtered many of its people

SOURCE 19

In November 1095, at a Church Council at Clermont in France, Pope Urban II urged the nobles and knights of Europe to fight to free the Holy Land from the Turks – whom he called *barbarians* (brutal, uncivilised people). A French chronicler, Fulcher of Chartres, was at the Council and reported the Pope's words as follows.

O Children of God … you should rapidly make an expedition to help your brothers who live in the East, who … have been invaded … by the Turks … Christ himself will be your leader … Wear his cross as your badge. If you are killed your sins will be pardoned … Let those who have been fighting against their own brothers and kinsfolk now fight lawfully against the barbarians.

SOURCE 18

Medieval pilgrims leaving the walled city of Canterbury. Only the well-to-do ones rode on horseback; most travelled on foot.

(**Source 21**). However Christians only held it until 1187, when the Turks recaptured the Holy Land. Their leader, Saladin, was merciful and generous in victory – unlike the Christians before him. There were several more crusades during the next hundred years, including one led by King Richard I of England. 'The Lionheart', as he was called, got to within sight of Jerusalem in 1192 but did not have enough forces left to attack it. None of the later crusades achieved any lasting success. Europe's 'holy wars' against the Muslims ended a costly failure.

SOURCE 21

An unknown French chronicler has left us this description of the massacre of Muslims and Jews inside Jerusalem, in July 1099.

Entering the city, our pilgrims pursued and killed Saracens (Turks) up to the temple of Solomon … so that their blood flowed throughout the temple. Finally … our knights seized a great number of men and women, and killed whom they wished … The crusaders ran through the city, seizing gold, silver, horses, mules and houses full of all kinds of goods. Then, rejoicing and weeping from extreme joy, our men went to worship … our Saviour Jesus and thus satisfied their promise to him.

Assessment tasks

A *Knowledge and understanding*

1 What changes in the English Church resulted from the Norman Conquest? In your answer, distinguish between (a) rapid changes and (b) gradual changes.

2 Using the information in Sources 7 and 13, compare the life of a Benedictine monk and a Franciscan friar. How were their lives similar and in what ways were they different?

3 Compare attitudes towards education in medieval times and today. What has changed and what has stayed the same? You should consider both (a) the subjects taught and (b) methods of teaching.

B *Interpretations and sources*

4 These modern writers on the Crusades present different views of Christ's wishes.

> That God could enjoin (preach) war was proved by the Old Testament … Moses had made war and Elijah had killed … It was true that the emphasis was different in the New [Testament], but, although Christ had preached forgiveness and meekness, he had, as St Luke related in his account of the Last Supper, also told the apostles to buy swords … Crusaders were called upon to deliver … the Holy Land from those who had seized it … The call to crusade was the right call for the time.
> (Louise and Jonathan Riley-Smith, 1981)

> Christ taught that all men should live together as brothers … But the Christians of the Middle Ages used the sword to spread a gospel that was supposed to carry a message of love and peace. The Crusades … brought little more than death, horror and misery to untold thousands of people.
> (Gerard Bell, 1966)

a In what ways are these accounts different? Can you suggest any reasons for the differences?
b Which of the two is closer to Pope Urban II's view of Christ's wishes (Source 19)? Give reasons for your answer.

5 Can you find any clues in Sources 7, 10 and 13 which help to explain why so many men and women were attracted to the monastic life in the Middle Ages?

6 Look again at Source 1.
a What do you think was the purpose of having pictures like this painted on the walls of medieval churches?
b What effect do you think such pictures would have had upon the parishioners?

4 Land and people
Farming and village life

Nowadays most British people live in towns and work in offices and factories. In medieval times there were no factories or machines and towns were tiny by modern standards. Nearly all the people lived in villages and farmed the land. Villages then were quite small, with perhaps twenty or thirty huts or cottages clustered round a stone church. Usually the only other stone building in the village was the lord's manor house. As we saw in Chapter 2, such villages were either manors or parts of manors controlled by one of the king's feudal tenants.

Peasants and their homes

The Normans called ordinary peasants *villeins* – from the French word *ville*, meaning a village or town. Some villeins were complete slaves (*serfs*); they had no land and worked all the time for the lord. However the majority of villeins had some land to farm and only worked part of the week for the lord. Even so, they were not free. They were the property of the lord, along with their homes and land, and forbidden to leave the manor without the lord's permission.

SOURCE 1

From the air, these grass fields in Northamptonshire reveal the place where the medieval village of Onley once stood. We can also see clearly the ridges from what was once ploughed land.

Villein families lived in huts with one or two rooms. These usually had a timber framework filled in with *wattle and daub* – plaited twigs smeared with mud. Roofs were thatched with straw or reeds. Inside, the floor of hard-trodden earth might be spread with rushes from the banks of the village stream. Windows were small and covered with rags or wooden shutters; glass was far too costly for peasants. This meant huts were dark in cold weather, when the windows were covered. They were smoky too, from the wood fire in the middle of the floor. As there was usually no chimney, smoke escaped as best it could through cracks and crevices (**Source 2**).

Furniture was home-made: stools, a table and a chest for clothes. Beds were bags of straw covered with woollen blankets. The women of the family spun and wove wool into rough cloth and made clothes. Almost everything villeins needed had to be made at home or by a village tradesman such as the blacksmith. The only essential goods brought in from outside were salt and iron. Otherwise each village was self-supporting. Most peasants never travelled more than a few miles from home as they had no means of transport.

Villeins' meals were very plain and changed little from day to day. Bread and cheese was the basic diet, perhaps flavoured with an onion and washed down with watery ale or cider. A little fish or salted meat was often added to the midday meal, with fruit in the summer. And when the day's work was over, hot *pottage* (vegetable soup) might be cooked in an iron pot. After each meal the wooden plates were probably wiped with grass.

SOURCE 2

This passage describes some of the discomforts of living in a peasant's hut. It has been translated into modern English from *Piers Plowman*, a long poem written in the fourteenth century by William Langland.

There are three things that would make a man run away from his own house ... One is a wicked wife who will not be corrected; her husband flees from her, for fear of her tongue. And if his house has no [proper] roof, and it rains on his bed, he searches far and wide until he finds a dry place to sleep. And when smoke and fumes sting his eyes, until he is bleary-eyed or blind, and his throat is hoarse ... it is even worse than his wife or a wet bed.

SOURCE 3

Open field farming depended on people respecting each other's rights. In some villages, *by-laws* (local rules) were made to discourage bad behaviour. Here are some by-laws from the Buckinghamshire village of Newton Longville, dating from 1290.

It is granted and ordered by the village community that in future no one shall gather green crops in another's corn field. Also that no one shall cause his beasts to graze among the corn in the night time. Also that no carting be done in the night time.
Also that everyone shall have his stiles and the lanes nearest him kept in good repair. And if anyone is found acting contrary ... he shall give the lord 6 pence. And if anyone is found offending at night he shall give the lord 12 pence.

'Open field' farming

The arrival of the Normans did not change English agriculture. Peasants carried on with farming methods that had been used for centuries. Over a large part of the country, especially in the Midlands and South, the village *arable* (ploughed) land was farmed in three big fields. These were 'open'; they did not have hedges or walls as farms do today. The land was given out to the villagers in narrow plots or strips. Each family's strips were scattered around all the fields, so each got its share of good and bad soil (**Source 3**).

Although each family looked after its own strips, villagers grouped together for some jobs, particularly ploughing (**Sources 4 and 5**). When the land had been ploughed corn crops were sown: possibly wheat or rye in one field in the autumn and barley in another in the spring. The third field was left *fallow* (unsown after ploughing). This was to give it a rest. If corn is grown on the same land every year, without fertilizer, the soil loses its goodness. Each field was left fallow one year out of three.

Leaving aside the lord's share, the rest of the land around the village was usually

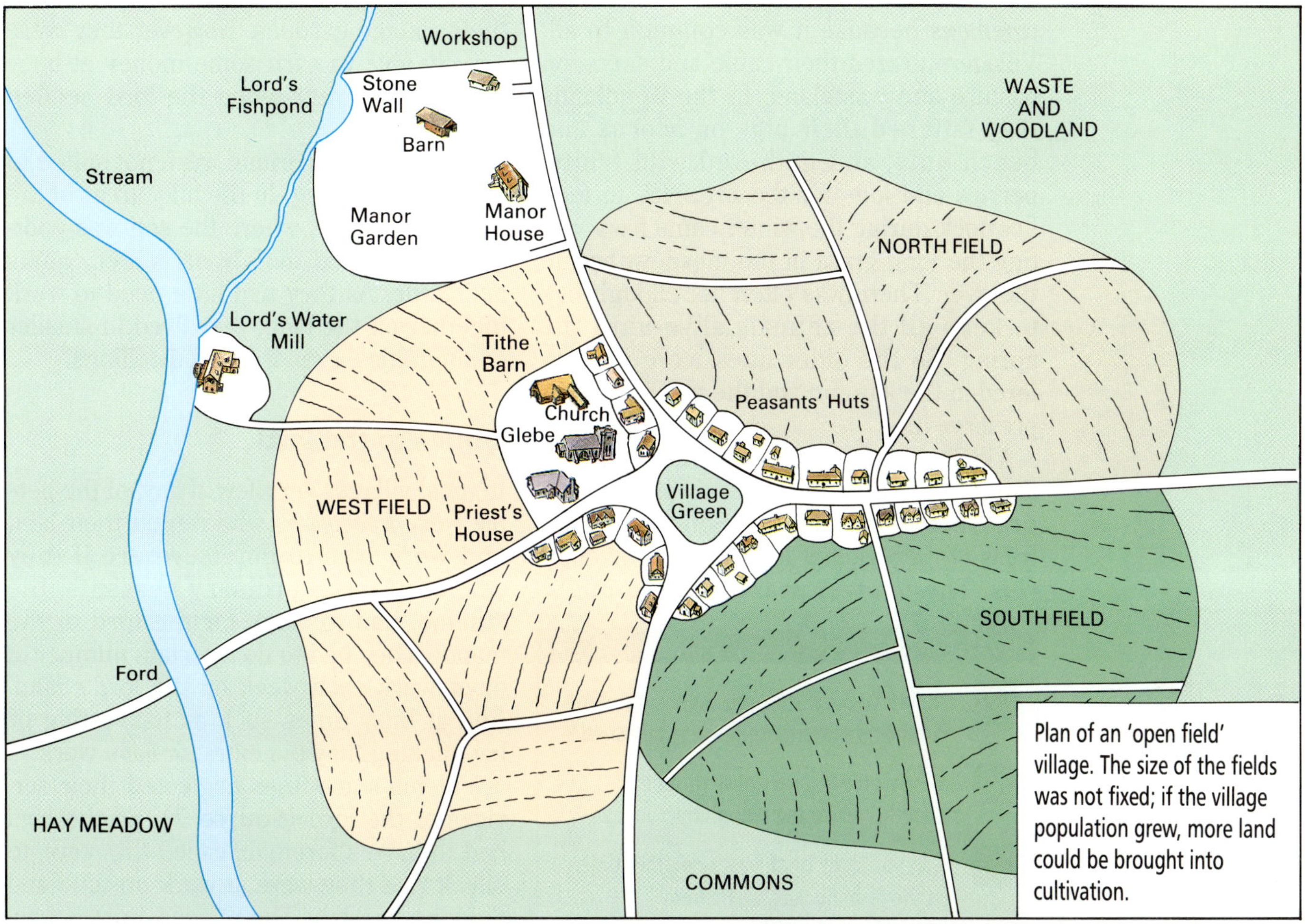

Plan of an 'open field' village. The size of the fields was not fixed; if the village population grew, more land could be brought into cultivation.

SOURCES 4 and 5

These illustrations from medieval manuscripts show how the plough was improved between the Norman Conquest and the fourteenth century. The first shows a simple wooden plough used in Norman England. In the second, which dates from about 1340, the plough is still mostly made of wood but its cutting parts (the *coulter* and the *share*) are made of iron. The large part by the ploughman's foot is the *mould-board*. It pushes the soil sideways and helps to make the furrow. Eight oxen (bullocks) might be needed to pull a plough through heavy soil, although teams of four or two could be used on lighter soils.

available to everyone. It was known as the *commons* because it was common to all. Villagers grazed their cattle and sheep on pasture and wasteland. In the woodlands they fattened their pigs on acorns and beech nuts, and gathered wild fruits, berries and logs for the fire. Hay to feed livestock during the winter came from cutting the long grass in the meadow, beside the river. There was often not enough hay to keep all the animals alive until the spring. So the older ones were slaughtered in the autumn and the meat salted to preserve it.

Villeins used the small gardens around their huts to grow vegetables such as peas, beans and onions. Some had fruit trees too, providing apples, pears or cherries. The poorest peasants, who might have no strips at all in the fields, relied on their cottage gardens. However they were usually able to earn some money at busy times of the year when the lord needed extra workers.

Many parts of Britain were not suited to open field farming. In the hilly areas of the North and West, where the soil was poorer, people lived mainly off sheep, goats and cattle. As they had little need to work together on the land, they lived in smaller communities, even isolated dwellings.

Duties to the lord

In most villages very few, if any, of the people were *freeholders* who rented their land and were free to go elsewhere if they wished. All the ordinary peasants, the villeins, had to work for the lord of the manor. They had to do a certain number of days' work each week on the lord's land. And at busy times such as harvesting or hay-making they did extra, or *boon* work.

Villeins sometimes neglected their services to the lord (**Source 7**). So the lord had to have a foreman, called the *reeve*, to check that they were at work on time and did jobs properly. The reeve, who was usually a villein himself, had to see that tools were in working order and ready when needed. He also made sure that farm

QUESTIONS

1. In Source 3, why do you think night-time offenders were more severely punished?
2. Why would villagers have grouped together to do the ploughing?
3. Can you think of at least one other time in the farming year, apart from ploughing, when villagers would have needed to work together?
4. At which times of year would a peasant's food stocks have been (a) lowest, and (b) highest? Give reasons for your answers.

SOURCE 6

Women harvesting corn with sickles. The one behind seems to have backache. The corn harvest was the busiest time of the year, when men, women and children all worked long hours. Like Source 5, on page 39, this comes from *The Luttrell Psalter* – a fourteenth-century book of psalms.

buildings and livestock were looked after. If a lord had several manors, he put each in charge of a *bailiff*, or manager. Bailiffs were free men and they had to be able to read and write because they kept the accounts of the manor.

As well as working on the lord's land, villeins had to give him some of their produce and pay him money at certain times (**Source 8**). They also had no choice but to grind their corn at the lord's mill and bake their bread in his ovens. Then the lord took some of the flour and bread as payment. A villein could not sell his livestock at market, nor give his daughter in marriage, without getting the lord's permission and paying him. And when a villein died his son or another member of his family had to pay for the right to take over his land.

Such matters were settled in the manor court, held by the lord or his chief official, the *steward* (**Source 10**). The manor court also dealt with wrongdoers who broke the customs of the manor. For example, a villein's cow might have been allowed to graze in the lord's meadow. If the owner was found guilty, by the freeholders or other responsible villagers, he or she had to pay a fine.

SOURCE 7

We know from manor records that villeins were often fined for failing to carry out their duties. Here is an example from the Yorkshire village of Methley in 1352.

Villeins of Methley ought and are accustomed to reap the corn of the lord in autumn ... [but] the aforesaid 53 villeins of Methley reaped only for nine and a half days ... so that a great part of the lord's oats growing there had been destroyed by a tempest of wind. Fined 17 shillings and 2 pence. Also the aforesaid 53 villeins of Methley ought and are accustomed to *scour* (clear out) a ditch called the Leighes. Through their failure the said meadows were flooded to the damage of the lord.

SOURCE 8

Here is part of a survey of the manor of Burton, in Staffordshire, made some time in the period 1114–18. It shows the kinds of services and payments villeins owed a lord. (*Pannage* was payment for feeding pigs in the woods).

In Burton ... the villeins are Fredebert, Edward, Adelon, Alwin, Leviet, Uctebrand, Eluric, Edric. Each ... works [for the lord] for 2 days each week. He must find a horse each year for the journey to the abbot's court or pay 3 pence. He must go for salt once, and for fish once, or give 2 pence for each carrying service. He must cart 1 cartload of wood. He must pay 2 hens at Christmas ... and give pannage. He must plough twice in the year, and ... anyone who between Pentecost [Whit] and August goes to the wood for a cartload of timber must pay 2 pence.

SOURCE 9

Peasants carry sacks of grain to the lord's mill – to be ground into flour by the miller. The water-wheel turns two big grindstones inside the mill. Before this, the grain had to be separated from the corn husk by *threshing* (beating) it with jointed sticks called flails.

SOURCE 10

Here are some extracts from the records of the manor court at Bradford in Yorkshire. The first dates from 1349; the others from 1354.

John Barne of Manningham, who held [a cottage and strips in the fields] is dead. And hereupon came Margery his wife and took those tenements (the dwelling and the strips) to hold according to the custom of the manor for the term of her life by the services, etc. And she gives to the lord 2 shillings of fine.

Agnes Chilyonge of Manningham, the lord's bondwoman (villein or serf), came here in Court and was fined 12 pence by the lord for her leyrwite (payment for becoming an unmarried mother) ... the fine is not more because she is very poor and has nothing.

Isabel, daughter of William Childyong, the lord's bondwoman, has married one William Cisson, a free man, without licence (the lord's permission). And Alice, daughter of John Gepson, the lord's bondwoman, has married one William del Hale, a free man, at Beston without licence; therefore let them be compelled to pay the lord a fine for their merchet (payment to get the lord's permission to marry).

SOURCE 11

A Norman manor house, at Boothby Pagnell in Lincolnshire. Notice the steps leading up to the main door on the first floor. The large square window was put in later. So was the chimney; originally the fireplace would have been in the middle of the hall floor and the smoke would have escaped through a hole in the roof.

Life in a manor house

Not all lords had grand homes. Some manor houses were quite small and built of wood on stone foundations. But in time most lords built stone houses, often protected by a high wall or moat. Like castle keeps, manor houses usually had a cellar on the ground floor and the main room, or hall, on the first floor, up a flight of steps (**Source 11**). Meals were eaten in the hall and at night the lord's servants slept there, on heaps of rushes or straw.

Next to the hall there was usually a private room, called the *bower*, where the lord's family slept. The lord's four-poster bed had curtains round it to keep out draughts. There were heavy wooden chests for clothes but no upholstered chairs. Carpets were rare. The kitchen was well away from the living quarters, because of the danger from its open fires. Next to it was the pantry, big enough to hold whole carcasses of meat. As manor houses grew larger, extra bedrooms were added and often a chapel. But only in the very richest homes were window-shutters replaced with glass.

At mealtimes, the lord, his family and other important people sat at the 'high table'. This stood on a small platform or *dais* (**Source 12**). Servants and others of lower rank had tables of their own. The butler laid knives and spoons but there were no table forks. Most eating was done with the fingers and bones were thrown on the floor where dogs waited to snap them up.

The two main meals of the day were dinner, at about noon, and supper in the early evening. The food at both was similar. After a bowl of vegetable soup, the main course might be boiled beef or mutton, roast pork or fish from a local river. It was a rule of the Church that fish should be eaten on Fridays. The meal ended with cheese and perhaps a fruit tart or pancakes. Ale was the usual drink, but if the lord had important guests French wine might be placed on the high table, with silver goblets.

SOURCE 12

This description of a feast in a manor house was written in the thirteenth century by a priest and teacher known as 'Bartholomew the Englishman'. (A 'board' is a trestle table. This has a separate top resting on wooden supports, making it easy to store away.)

Guests are sat with the lord in the chief place of the board, and they sit not down at the board before they wash their hands. Children are sat in their place, and servants at a table by themselves. First knives, spoons and salts are set on the board, and then bread and drink and many different dishes ... The guests are gladdened with lutes and harps. Now wine and dishes of meat are brought forth and divided. At the last comes fruit and spices, and when they have eaten ... guests wash and wipe their hands again.

QUESTIONS

1. Why do you think manor houses were often similar in design to castle keeps?
2. In Source 12, can you explain why the guests needed to wash their hands so often?
3. What would have been the advantage of having trestle tables in the hall of a manor house?
4. Try to find out why the Church ruled that fish, not meat, should be eaten on Fridays.

For big feasts on special occasions, the lord's servants might roast a whole pig or poultry such as goose, duck or pheasant. A travelling acrobat or jester was sometimes hired to entertain the guests, while minstrels sang and played in a raised gallery. When darkness fell the hall was lit by tall wax candles or flaming torches stuck in iron holders round the walls. The men usually carried on drinking long after the ladies had gone to bed.

Pastimes and festivals

The lord of the manor might entertain his guests by taking them hunting. If there were no deer or wild boar in the woods nearby, foxes, hares or badgers would be tracked down with a pack of dogs. Meanwhile, in the manor house the lord's wife would give instructions to the servants and the children would have lessons in French and Latin. Often the teacher was the village priest.

After lessons the lord's children would play games. They had hoops, tops, skipping ropes and board games such as chess and draughts. Older boys often went horse-riding or practised archery. Their sisters learned to sing, dance and do embroidery. Girls were often married in their early teens, to husbands chosen by

SOURCE 13

The lord of the manor's high table. This scene from *The Luttrell Psalter* shows the owner of the book, Sir Geoffrey Luttrell himself, at dinner. Instead of plates, slices of stale bread called *trenchers* were put out. Notice the trestle table (see Source 12).

SOURCE 14

The popular sport of hawking (hunting with hawks) is shown in this French picture. The lord's falconer trained hawks to perch on the wrist until a suitable prey appeared, such as a wild duck or heron.

their parents. Marriage 'for love' was rare in well-to-do families.

Peasant children probably had little time for play. They looked after the family's animals, fetched water from the well or stream and did odd jobs. However on Sundays and summer evenings they would play tag or blind man's buff and make swings and see-saws. Adults enjoyed dancing on the village green and family celebrations such as weddings or christenings. Weddings were often an excuse for heavy drinking, despite the disapproval of the church (**Source 16**).

SOURCE 15

This fourteenth-century illustration shows one of the games that people played on the village green. It is based on a Greek pastime called *Hippas*. Can you describe what is happening in the picture?

Village festivals were held regularly. Some were linked to the seasons. For example, in springtime the villagers celebrated the end of the long, dark winter. On 1 May they danced round a maypole and crowned two young people with flowers as King and Queen of the May. Most festivals were holy days (holidays) of the Church. Altogether there were about fifty such days in the year, but on most manors work only stopped on about fifteen to twenty of them – mainly around Easter, Whit and Christmas (**Source 17**).

SOURCE 16

Here the Bishop of Durham, in 1220, confirms the Church's teaching on marriage. It seems that the Christian idea of marriage was often abused.

We order that marriages be decently celebrated, with reverence, not with laughter and ribaldry (foul language), not in taverns or at public drinkings and feastings. Let no man place a ring made of rushes or of any material, worthless or precious, on the hand of a woman in jest (as a joke) that he may more easily gain her favours … In future let no promise of marriage be given except in the presence of a priest.

SOURCE 17

At Christmas, some lords held a feast for the villagers in the manor house. Others gave out a *gestum* – food and drink to take home which included enough for guests. This is what one villager in North Curry, Somerset, was entitled to in 1314.

John of Knapp … shall have … his gestum at Christmas with two others, namely two white loaves, as much beer as they will drink in the day, a mess (serving) of beef and of bacon with mustard, one of browis of hen (chicken broth), and a cheese, fuel to cook his food … and to burn from dinner time till evening and afterwards, and two candles of the usual size to burn out while they sit and drink.

Assessment tasks

A *Knowledge and understanding*

1 The word villein (now spelt villain) has come to mean a wrongdoer. From reading this chapter (including the sources), can you see any reasons why it got this meaning?

2 In what ways would a medieval manor house have been less comfortable to live in than most modern houses? Give as many details as you can. Are there any ways in which it might have been *more* comfortable?

3 Why do you think well-to-do parents in medieval times arranged the marriages of their children?

B *Interpretations and sources*

4 Below is a modern artist's impression of medieval peasants in their cottage garden. It appeared in a children's history book published in 1971.

a How far do you think the details in the picture are historically accurate? Give reasons for your answer.

b Compare this picture with similar modern illustrations of peasants in school library books. Can you explain why there are often big differences between them?

5 From the sources in this chapter, find as many examples as you can of ways in which lords treated peasants as their property.

6 What can we say about the former village of Onley from the evidence in Source 1?

The cottage garden

5 A King governs

The English Monarchy under Henry II

On 19 December 1154, a confident and strong-willed young man of twenty-one was crowned King Henry II at Westminster Abbey. Wearing long robes, like a priest, he stood at the altar while the Archbishop of Canterbury *anointed* (smeared) him with holy oil. Henry, like all medieval Christian kings, was believed to have God-given powers and to be God's representative on earth.

We know a lot about Henry II, from books written by members of the royal household. All agree that he was a man of great energy and, like his grandfather Henry I, a strong and skilful ruler. He seems to have been friendly, witty and generous. He had a quick temper and sometimes flew into a rage, but he did not show the harshness and cruelty of the Conqueror and his sons (**Source 1**).

As well as England, Henry ruled more than half of France. From his father, Geoffrey, Count of Anjou, he inherited large parts of northern France. Lands further south, stretching as far as the Spanish border, came to him from his marriage, at the age of eighteen, to Eleanor, Countess of Aquitaine. She was a lively and determined woman, more than ten years older than the King.

SOURCE 1

This view of Henry II was written by Walter Map, who lived in the royal household. Walter served for a time as one of Henry's judges and later became an archdeacon.

Henry … was a little over medium height, a man blessed with sound limbs and a handsome face … In bodily skill he was second to none … he had a knowledge of every language spoken from the coasts of France to the Jordan (Palestine), although he only used Latin and French. He was skilful in making laws and running his government … On the other hand, he was always on the move, travelling in unbearably long stages … and in this he showed little thought for his household which went with him. He had great experience of hounds and hawks and was a very keen follower of that sport (hunting); he was wakeful at night and always working.

SOURCE 2

A silver penny of Henry II. Henry of Anjou – as he was known in his youth – was the first of a long line of 'Plantagenet' kings, so-called because his father's badge was the yellow broom flower (*planta genesta* in Latin).

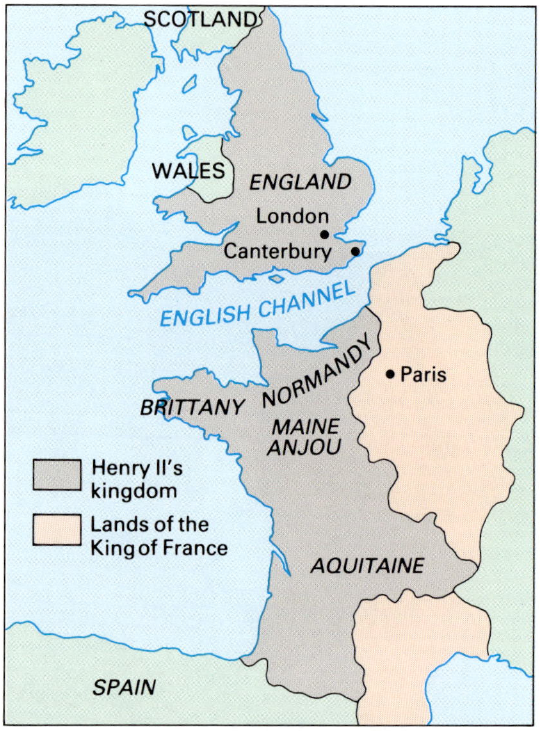

Henry II's empire. He inherited England and Normandy from his mother, Anjou and Maine from his father, and Aquitaine from his wife. Brittany was gained after he became king.

Henry takes control

Henry II needed all his energy and strength to deal with England's troubles. Ever since the death of his grandfather, in 1135, the barons had been fighting each other. Henry I left, as heir to the throne, a daughter called Matilda – Henry II's mother. But a large group of barons would not accept a woman ruler. They supported Henry I's nephew, Count Stephen, who was crowned king. Matilda stood up for her rights, backed by a number of barons. The result was civil war. Not until Stephen died, childless, in 1154, was there a monarch everyone could accept – Matilda's son Henry.

The young King's first task was to restore law and order. During Stephen's reign many barons had built castles without royal permission and kept their own private armies. They had robbed and murdered without being brought to justice. Henry gave orders to destroy about 300 castles. He also sent home the *mercenaries* (foreign soldiers) who had been hired on the Continent to fight for either Stephen or Matilda.

Methods of recruiting royal armies were changing. Most of the king's wars now took place in France, so there was less need to have thousands of knights at the ready in England. Many barons preferred to make a payment called *scutage* (shield money) to the king instead of providing knights. With the money the king hired soldiers in France when he needed them. Knights now often gave up being professional soldiers and concentrated on looking after their manors. As a result England grew more peaceful.

The royal household

Nowadays the government is run from London. Laws are prepared and carried out by thousands of people in offices along Whitehall – the road leading from Trafalgar Square to the Houses of Parliament. In medieval times, however, there were no telephones, computers or other modern methods of communication. The king had to keep moving around his kingdom to hear complaints from his subjects, judge disputes and check up on royal officials. As he rode on horseback from one manor or castle to the next, a large household travelled with him. This included all sorts of people, from powerful barons to humble cooks and bed-makers (**Source 3**).

The kingdom was ruled from wherever the king was staying. The leading members of his household not only looked after his personal affairs but also helped him to govern. The most important was the chancellor, in charge of the king's private chapel. The clerks (priests) who worked

SOURCE 3

Life in Henry II's court is described in this letter written by Peter of Blois, a Frenchman invited to England by the King.

I often wonder how anyone ... can put up with the annoyances of court life ... The beer at court is horrid to taste and filthy to look at. Because of the great demand, meat is sold whether it is fresh or not. The fish one buys is four days old ... Indeed the tables are sometimes filled with rotting food ... If the king has decided to stay anywhere for the day ... you may be sure that he will get off somewhere else early in the morning, and by his sudden change of mind upset everybody's plans; men run about like mad, urging on the packhorses, driving carts into one another, and everything is in a state of confusion.

SOURCE 4

Wherever the king went, his servants had to pack clothes, food, furniture, cooking utensils and the rest of the equipment of the household. Luggage too heavy for packhorses was carried in carts like the one pictured here. Carts often got stuck, however, as the roads were just rough tracks.

SOURCE 5

Henry II's Great Seal pressed on sealing wax. The impression was made with a hollow mould which had the design cut inside. What do you think the objects in the King's hands are meant to stand for?

SOURCE 6

One of the marshal's duties was to pay the servants. This record of wages paid to members of the royal household dates from 1136; things would have been much the same under Henry II. The wages seem very small to us, but at that time a labourer could live on as little as a penny a day.

The watchmen shall have double food rations, three halfpence a day for their men and four candles … The stoker of the fire shall always live in the king's household, and from Michaelmas (29 September) until Easter he shall have fourpence a day for the fire. The usher of the chamber shall have fourpence for the king's bed every day the king is travelling … Each of four hornblowers shall have threepence a day … the bowman who carries the king's bow shall have fivepence a day.

SOURCE 7

Servants working in a medieval kitchen (pictured in *The Luttrell Psalter*). The man roasting fowl and a small pig over a fire was called the turnspit. Notice also the man above pounding ingredients in a bowl called a mortar.

under the chancellor had the task of writing the king's official letters and documents. The king did not sign these. Instead, a blob of sealing wax was attached to them and stamped with his Great Seal (**Source 5**).

Other leading members of the household included the marshal, in charge of the horses and hunting dogs, (**Source 6**) and the steward and master-butler who were responsible for getting the food and cooking it. In the royal *chamber* (bedroom) servants under the orders of the master-chamberlain looked after the king's bed, his clothes and valuables. One of these, the *ewerer* (water-bearer), filled the king's bath and dried his clothes when he got wet.

Under the Norman kings (from William I to Stephen) a very important member of the royal household was the treasurer. He collected the taxes, rents and other money due to the king. Under Henry II, however, the treasurer no longer travelled around with the king. It was easier for him to stay in London, in the *Exchequer* – named after its counting table spread with a chequered cloth. Sheriffs collected the king's money in their counties. Twice a year they travelled to London to make their payments to the Exchequer (**Source 8**).

To discuss matters such as new laws or taxes, the king called together his great council. Barons, bishops and other tenants-in-chief had to travel to wherever the king happened to be. However, many decisions had to be taken in the king's absence because he was often in France looking after his lands there. Indeed, for every year of his reign that Henry spent in England, he spent nearly two years in France. While he was away, his *justiciar* (chief justice), acted as deputy.

Law and order

On his travels, Henry judged disputes between his subjects and punished wrongdoers. He was helped in the task of keeping law and order by a team of royal justices. Some were based in the palace of Westminster, in London. Others travelled round the kingdom holding courts, known as *assizes*, in each county. Similar courts had been held from time to time in the reign of Henry I. Henry II made them a regular part of the English legal system.

When the king's travelling judges arrived in a county, the sheriff gathered what was called a *jury of presentment*. This was made up of twelve trusted men from the neighbourhood who swore to accuse honestly those suspected of wrongdoing. Such juries were different from a modern trial jury which listens to evidence and then comes to a decision. Juries of presentment had to decide who they would accuse before coming to court.

Only God, it was believed, really knew whether an accused person was guilty or not. So God was asked to give a sign in a special kind of trial called an *ordeal*. This was carried out by a priest, using either water or iron. In the ordeal by water the most common method was to lower the accused by a rope into a pond or river. It was believed that the water would 'receive' the innocent, who sank, and reject the guilty, who floated (**Source 10**). The ordeal by iron was a 'burn test'. The accused carried a piece of red-hot iron a short distance. If the burnt hand festered it was a sign of guilt.

Such ordeals had been used for centuries. But by Henry II's time people were beginning to lose faith in this kind of trial. The King would have preferred to see judgements based on evidence and the reputation of the accused. But he knew how difficult it would be to break completely with the past. He therefore ruled that if a man accused of a serious offence was cleared by the ordeal he must still be banished from the kingdom (**Source 12**).

SOURCE 8

This description of the Exchequer was written by Henry II's treasurer, Richard fitz Nigel, in about 1179. Sheriffs often tried to keep for themselves some of the money they owed the king. So the barons of the Exchequer studied the accounts very carefully.

The exchequer is a rectangular board, about ten feet long and five wide, used as a table by those who sit at it. A raised edge, about the height of four fingers, runs round it to prevent anything placed on it from falling off. Over the board is spread a cloth ... marked like a chess-board ... Within the spaces, counters are placed according to their value ... Just as in chess the battle is fought between kings, here it is chiefly between ... the treasurer and the sheriff, who sits with his accounts before him while the others sit like judges to watch.

SOURCE 9

The amount of money a sheriff paid into the Exchequer was recorded by means of cuts or notches in a stick of wood called a *tally*. Tallies were split down the middle and the sheriff and the Exchequer each kept half. If there was any dispute later about how much had been paid, the two halves could be put together and made to 'tally'.

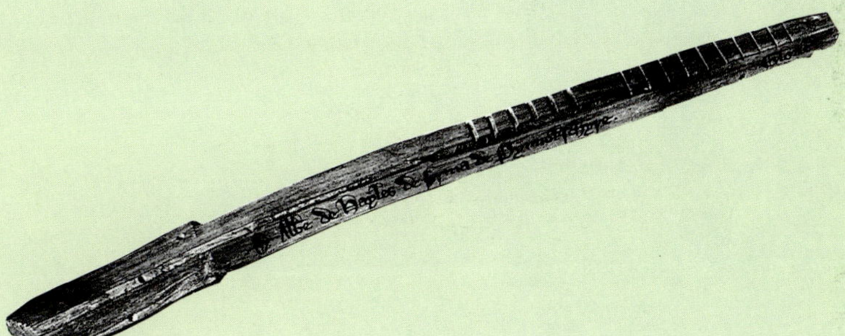

SOURCE 10

The ordeal by water, described here in a medieval document, was the method of trial commonly used for villeins and serfs. Freemen were often given a burn test.

Let the hands of the accused be bound together under the bent knees ... Then he shall be bound around the waist with a rope strong enough to hold him; and in the rope will be made a knot at the distance of the length of his hair; and so he shall be let down gently into the water so as not to make a splash. If he sinks down to the knot he shall be drawn up and saved; otherwise let him be judged a guilty man by the spectators.

SOURCE 11

The Court of King's Bench – one of several royal courts – pictured in the early fifteenth century. The five judges are at the top; below are the clerks, with parchment rolls, pen cases and ink, and (on the left) the jury. Can you find the prisoner on trial, and also the others waiting to come before the court?

In 1215 the Pope, Innocent III, stopped priests from taking part in ordeals. This soon put an end to them. From then on members of the jury were asked whether or not they thought the accused was guilty and evidence became important. Henry did not live to see this happen, but he did much to prepare the way.

SOURCE 12

This is part of the Assize of Northampton – a series of royal *decrees* (commands which had to be obeyed as laws) issued by Henry II in 1176.

If anyone has been accused before the king's justices of murder or theft or robbery, or of sheltering men who commit such crimes, or of forgery or arson … let him go to the ordeal of water, and if he fail, let him … lose his right hand with his foot … And if he shall be cleared of guilt at the water, let him … remain in the kingdom, unless he has been accused of murder or some other serious offence by the general opinion … If he has been accused in this way … let him leave the kingdom within forty days.

QUESTIONS

1. Why do you think King Henry's treasurer found it easier to stay in London than to travel with the royal household?
2. What was the purpose of having so many men in a jury? Why was it not left to just one person to accuse suspected wrongdoers?
3. In the Court of King's Bench (Source 11) the man standing in front of the jury is holding a large book. What do you think he is doing?
4. What is the difference between a robber and a thief? Why do you think it would have been hard to prevent crimes of this sort in the Middle Ages?

Relations with the Church – the quarrel with Becket

Not all the thousands of churchmen in Henry's kingdom lived holy lives. Some were caught breaking the law. When this happened, they had the right to be tried in one of the Church's own courts. Punishments in these courts were lighter than in the king's courts. For example, a church court could not give the death sentence, even for murder. The worst that could happen to a guilty churchman was to be *excommunicated* (expelled from the Church). If, after that, he was found guilty of another crime he would suffer the normal punishment.

This did not satisfy Henry. He wanted church courts to hand over all men found guilty of serious crimes to ordinary courts so that they could be punished properly (**Source 13**). Most bishops were against this idea, but Henry hoped to get support from Thomas Becket, Archbishop of Canterbury and head of the English Church. Before becoming Archbishop in 1162, Becket had been Henry's Chancellor and a close friend; the two had spent many happy hours hunting and hawking together. Henry had helped to get his friend appointed Archbishop, even though Becket did not seem particularly religious.

SOURCE 13

In January 1164, Henry II held a council of nobles in the royal hunting lodge at Clarendon, near Salisbury. He insisted on making the following ruling, even though the bishops disagreed with it.

Clerks (churchmen) accused of any crime shall, when ordered by the king's justice, come before the king's court ... concerning matters which seem to be answerable there, and before the church court for what seems to be answerable there ... The king's justice shall find out the result of the trial in the church court. And if the clerk is convicted or confesses his guilt, the Church ought no longer to protect him.

SOURCE 14

This is the earliest known picture of the murder of Thomas Becket, on 29 December 1170 (see page 52). It was drawn fifty years after his death. Written accounts by eyewitnesses confirm that he was killed by sword blows on the top of his head.

On becoming Archbishop, Becket changed completely. He stayed up far into the night praying and reading the Bible. He lived on bread and water and wore next to his skin a rough shirt of goats' hair, swarming with fleas and lice. Becket refused any longer to do what Henry wanted. He said his first duty was to the Church and that he could not accept the King's ruling on church courts. This, he said, would mean punishing a man twice for the same offence. A bitter quarrel broke out between the King and Becket which lasted six years. Henry stubbornly refused to give way and Becket fled to the Continent.

The quarrel seemed to have been patched up in 1170 and Becket returned to England. But straightaway he excommunicated some of the King's supporters. When the news reached Henry, in Normandy, he flew into a rage and shouted, 'Will nobody rid me of this troublesome priest?' Four knights took him at his word. Secretly, they made their way to Canterbury. Becket's servants made him go into the cathedral for safety, but the knights, wearing armour, clattered after him. They tried to drag him outside but he clung to a pillar. Suddenly the knights attacked him savagely with their swords. Becket fell to the ground dead, the top of his head almost sliced off.

SOURCE 15

Gervase, a monk of Canterbury, witnessed Henry II's pilgrimage to Thomas Becket's tomb in 1174. This is how he described it.

The king … walked barefoot and dressed in a woollen smock [from outside Canterbury] all the way to the martyr's tomb. There he lay flat out for a long while in humble devotion, and allowed himself to be whipped by all the bishops and abbots present and all the monks of the church of Canterbury. There he remained, praying without a break before the holy martyr all that day and night.

The whole of Christendom was shocked by Becket's death. He was *canonised* (made a saint) by the Pope and pilgrims from many countries flocked to worship at his tomb in Canterbury Cathedral. The King, meanwhile, deeply regretted his angry words and begged the Pope for forgiveness. In 1174 Henry visited Becket's tomb to show his sorrow (**Source 15**). He gave up his attempt to reform the church courts. No other medieval king even tried.

The invasion of Ireland

While the quarrel with Becket was coming to its unhappy end, events in Ireland demanded the King's attention. To most people in Europe, the Irish were a backward and quarrelsome people. They were not united under a single ruler but divided into a number of warring kingdoms. Bands of bearded warriors, in black woollen clothing, fought each other with spears, axes and sling-stones.

The medieval Irish Kingdoms.

By Henry II's time, Norman barons advancing from England had conquered south Wales. Some were keen to further their ambitions in Ireland. In the years 1169–70, a band of Norman lords sailed to Ireland and seized the ports of Wexford, Waterford and Dublin. Chief among them, with 1200 men, was Richard, Earl of Pembroke – nicknamed 'Strongbow'. He had been invited to help the King of Leinster, Dermot MacMurrough, fight his enemies. In return, he was given Dermot's daughter, Eva, in marriage. Within a year Dermot had died and Strongbow was master of Leinster.

Strongbow's growing power alarmed King Henry. He was determined not to stand by and allow one of his barons to become a king in his own right. So in October 1171 Henry landed near Waterford with 4000 men. Strongbow and the other Norman lords immediately did *homage* to him (see page 19). So did most of the Irish kings. Henry took the title 'Lord of Ireland'. Strongbow was allowed to remain in Leinster until his death in 1176.

Henry did not try to conquer the whole of Ireland. He seemed more interested in pleasing the Pope by making some changes the Pope wanted in the Irish Church. It was Henry's chance to get back in favour with Church leaders after the murder of Becket. Without delay, he called a council of Irish bishops at Cashel. The Irish Church was brought into line with the rest of Christendom by being organised into dioceses and parishes. Also the Irish agreed to pay tithes and to make their marriages, baptisms and other church services like those in England (**Source 17**).

SOURCE 16

Dunbrody Abbey, in County Wexford – one of over thirty monasteries built by the Cistercians in Ireland in the twelfth and thirteenth centuries.

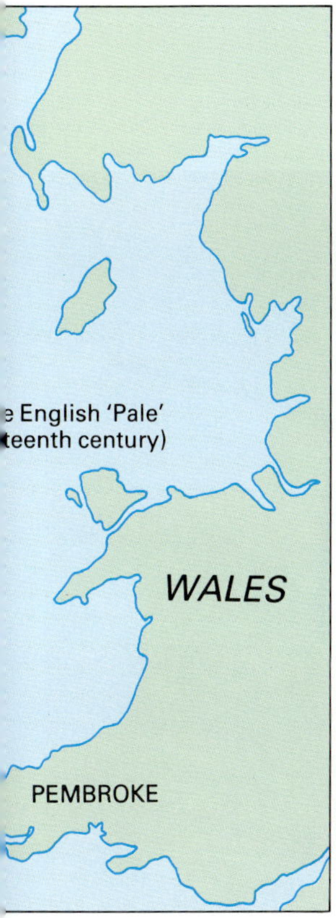

QUESTIONS

1. What is a martyr? Why was Thomas Becket considered to be one?
2. Look again at Source 14. Why do you think the artist shows the murder taking place beside an altar and a priest with a cross?
3. What is Lent? Why did the Pope (Source 17) disapprove of those who ate meat at this time?
4. Have you remembered from Chapter 3 what tithes are? Why would the Pope (Source 17) have wanted the Irish to pay tithes?

English kings after Henry II added to their Irish lands until, by 1300, they controlled about two-thirds of the island. They put up castles for defence and encouraged the building of churches and abbeys. But Ireland remained only partly conquered. In the later Middle Ages descendants of the Norman barons quarrelled among themselves and English control of Ireland was reduced. English law was in force only in the area round Dublin, known as the *Pale*. 'Beyond the Pale' there was still much disorder.

SOURCE 17

The Pope, Alexander III, was delighted with the reforms in the Irish Church brought about by Henry II. In 1172 he wrote to thank him.

Alexander … to his dearest son in Christ, Henry … When we heard … that you had assembled a mighty force by sea and land to subject this people [the Irish] to your rule … we were duly thankful … All of them eat meat during Lent; they do not pay tithes; and they do not respect, as they should, either the churches of God or the clergymen who serve them … We bid you to strengthen and renew your purpose to bring back this people to the worship of Christ.

SOURCE 18

Henry II died in 1189. This likeness is on his tomb at the abbey church of Fontevrault in central France. His last years were clouded by family quarrels. His sons sided with the King of France and fought against their father. It was left to members of his household to mourn his death. 'Everybody loved him', said Peter of Blois, 'because he called for strict justice and made peace'.

Assessment tasks

A *Knowledge and understanding*

1 What changes occurred in Henry II's reign to make England more peaceful and its people more law-abiding? What further changes of this kind might Henry have made if he had got his way?

2 Write down what you think were the reasons for the ending of trial by ordeal in the thirteenth century. Which *one* of these reasons do you consider the most important?

3 What were the consequences of the death of Thomas Becket? You should be able to think of quite a number. Distinguish between those that were:

a *religious* (to do with worship and the affairs of the Church);
b *political* (affecting those in power – especially the King).

B *Interpretations and sources*

4 Here are two views of Thomas Becket written by historians in the twentieth century.

> [After] this cowardly crime ... Becket became a saint and a martyr, and thousands visited his tomb. [There was] horror ... at the tragic death of a sincere and fearless champion of the Church's cause.
> (J.E. Williams & H. Sidney Warwick, 1906)

> The martyrdom of Thomas Becket was a martyrdom which he had repeatedly gone out of his way to seek ... one cannot but feel sympathy towards Henry, thus placed in a position of responsibility for the death of a man who in happier days had, after all, been his friend. Becket got what he asked for.
> (John Harvey, 1948)

a Which of these views would most people in the Middle Ages have agreed with? Give reasons for your answer.
b Why do you think there is such disagreement about Becket?
c Which side are you on, and why?

5 Re-read Sources 1, 3 and 6.

a Overall, what kind of picture do these sources present of the King's daily life?
b Judging from these sources, how well do you think the King treated his servants and officials?

6 What do Sources 13, 15 and 17 tell you about Henry II's attitude towards the Church?

6 Baronial rebellion

Magna Carta and the beginning of Parliament

Henry II's youngest son, John, has often been described as England's worst ever king. Certainly he had a very unpleasant side to his character. He was cruel, greedy, untrustworthy and quick-tempered. But as a ruler John also had good qualities. He worked hard to govern his kingdom – unlike his older brother, Richard I (1189–99), who ruled before him. Richard spent all but six months of his reign away from England fighting wars. John, on the other hand, regularly visited all parts of his kingdom, judging legal cases, holding meetings of his council and keeping a watch on the work of royal officials.

One reason for John's bad reputation is that he suffered heavy defeats in battle. It was difficult for a medieval king to gain respect if he failed as a war leader. Another important reason was that he quarrelled with the Pope. This made him unpopular with churchmen – at a time when history was still written mainly by monks. One monk, Roger of Wendover, wrote a chronicle of John's reign which blackened his character. Roger's views were copied by later writers, including one of the best known medieval chroniclers, Matthew Paris (**Source 2**). For centuries afterwards, historians believed many exaggerated stories about John.

SOURCE 1

An *effigy* (likeness) of King John on his tomb in Worcester Cathedral. John chose to be buried in Worcester near the tomb of his favourite saint, Wulfstan.

'John Softsword'

King John was also very unlucky. Throughout his reign of seventeen years (1199–1216) he faced a strong and skilful enemy, King Philip II of France. Philip was determined to conquer John's French lands. He had already fought long wars against Richard I, but 'the Lionheart' was a great warrior and hard to beat. When Richard died suddenly, from a septic wound, Philip saw his chance and prepared for a fresh attack.

At first things went well for John. Marching an army 80 miles in 48 hours, he surprised the French and seized the castle of Mirebeau. To his delight, he found he had captured his teenage nephew, Arthur, Count of Brittany, who was on Philip's side. Arthur was thrown in prison and never seen again. We do not know for sure what happened to him, but it seems likely that he was murdered by John (**Source 3**).

Before long, many of John's French subjects were flocking to join Philip, who won

SOURCE 2

This view of King John was written by Matthew Paris (1200–59), a monk of the abbey of St Albans in Hertfordshire. Roger of Wendover, who died in 1236, was also a monk at St Albans.

John was a tyrant not a king, a destroyer instead of a ruler, crushing his own people and favouring foreigners ... He lost the duchy of Normandy and many other territories through laziness ... He forced money out of his subjects and was never satisfied; he invaded and destroyed his subjects' property; and he bred no worthy children but only such as took after their father. He detested his wife and she him ... As for the Christian religion, he was lacking in faith.

SOURCE 3

The monks of the abbey of Margam in Wales wrote this account of Arthur's death. They probably got the story from their local baron, William de Briouze, who had actually captured Arthur.

After King John had captured Arthur and kept him alive in prison for some time, at length, in the castle of Rouen, after dinner on the Thursday before Easter [3 April 1203], when he was drunk and possessed by the devil, he killed him with his own hands, and tying a heavy stone to the body threw it into the river Seine. It was found by a fisherman in his net, and, after being dragged to the bank and recognised, it was buried secretly.

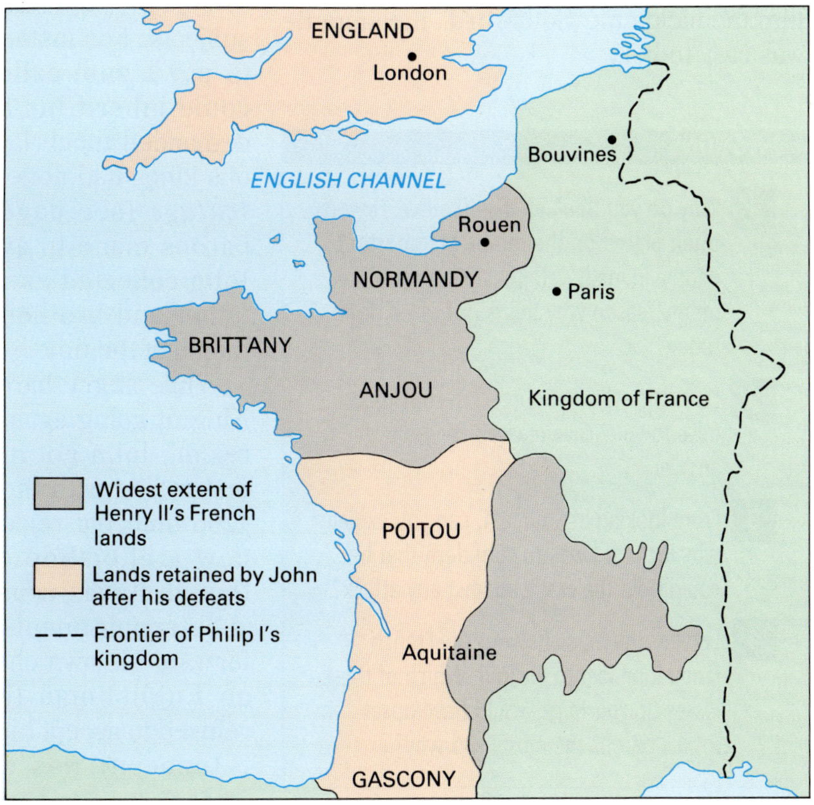

France in the time of John and Philip II. John lost two-thirds of his French lands to Philip.

SOURCE 4

The ruins of *Chateau Gaillard*. The name is French for Saucy Castle. Richard I had it built (1198) like the Crusader castles he had seen in the Holy Land. Philip II once swore he would capture it even if its walls were made of iron. Richard replied that he would hold it even if they were made of butter!

a string of victories. In 1204 he captured *Chateau Gaillard*, a castle built on a cliff above the river Seine which Richard I had boasted was unconquerable (**Source 4**). This was followed by the conquest of the whole of Normandy, Brittany and Anjou. It was a staggering blow which turned many of John's barons against him. They gave him the nickname 'Softsword', meaning he was easy to beat.

QUESTIONS

1. Why do you think *effigies* (Source 1) were often placed on the tombs of important people in medieval times? Can you think of any reason why this is not often done today?
2. Does the story in Source 3 seem true or false to you? Give reasons for your answer.
3. From looking at Source 4, can you explain why Richard I was so confident that he could hold the castle against any attack?
4. Look at the map showing the French lands John lost to Philip II. Which of these losses do you think would have upset John's barons the most, and why?

Quarrels with barons and the Church

John never gave up hope of getting his French lands back. But he needed money to fight another war against Philip and his attempts to get it made him many enemies. As feudal lord, the King was entitled to certain payments from his wealthier subjects. For instance, a baron's son had to pay a sum called a *relief* before he could inherit his father's estates. John demanded much larger reliefs than previous kings had done. He did the same with *scutage* (see page 47) – the payment barons made to avoid military service. John collected as many scutages as his father and brother put together, in less than half the time.

While angry barons were accusing the King of going against the 'customs of the realm', John got into further trouble by quarrelling with the Pope, Innocent III. In 1206 Innocent rejected John's choice of a new archbishop of Canterbury, even though it was usual for kings to decide such appointments. When Innocent put forward his own choice, Stephen Langton, an Englishman living in Rome, John refused to accept him.

Innocent was determined that the

Church should be respected. In 1208 he put England under an *interdict*, which meant that all the churches had to be kept locked (**Source 6**). This caused great distress at a time when religion meant so much to people, but John seemed in no hurry to settle the quarrel. He even forced a number of churchmen who criticised him to leave England. Innocent was furious and *excommunicated* the King (expelled him from the Church).

John did not give in until 1213. At a special ceremony he 'gave' England to the Church and agreed to rule it in the Pope's name. John also accepted Stephen Langton as Archbishop. Innocent was delighted and from that time became very friendly towards the King. The interdict was ended, but the damage to John's reputation could not be repaired. To churchmen, a king who was excommunicated could be nothing but evil.

SOURCE 5

Drawing of the Seal of Archbishop Stephen Langton. What is he holding in his left hand, and can you explain its meaning to Christians?

The Great Charter

In the summer of 1214, John joined forces with Otto IV, emperor of Germany, aiming to recover his French lands. John had an early success when he captured the port of Nantes. But his French barons refused to fight and he was forced to retreat. Then King Philip destroyed Otto's army at Bouvines in Flanders (now Belgium) (**Source 7**). This disaster gave John's enemies the chance they had been waiting for. A powerful group of barons demanded that he listen to their complaints. When John refused, they gathered an army in Lincolnshire, marched south and captured London.

SOURCE 6

Most church services were forbidden by the Pope's *interdict* (prohibition) of 1208–14. This account was written by Roger of Wendover.

The bishops, finding the King unwilling to repent ... carried out the duty asked of them by the Pope ... On 23 March ... all church services stopped in England, except for the confession of sins, communion for the dying and the baptism of children. The bodies of the dead were carried out of cities and towns, and buried in roads and ditches without prayers or the attendance of priests.

John was taken by surprise. He had no money to hire soldiers, so he fled to Windsor castle and agreed to meet the barons to hear their complaints. The meeting took place at Runnymede, a field beside the river Thames between Staines and Windsor, on 15 June 1215. Discussions went on for several days. Then everything the King had promised was written down in a document known as the *Magna Carta* (Latin for Great Charter). John put his seal on it and copies were sent to every sheriff in the country.

Magna Carta was about laws and customs the barons said the King had broken or ignored. It was granted to all freemen of the realm (not villeins), but the barons gained most from it. In future John was not to ask for scutage until the barons had agreed to it. And relief payments were set at £100 (some barons had paid several

SOURCE 7

This illustration from the *Chronicles* of Matthew Paris shows the battle of Bouvines, July 1214. It was a confused battle, fought in a dust storm. Here we see King Philip falling from his horse while one of John's supporters, Hugh de Burgh, rides away.

SOURCE 8

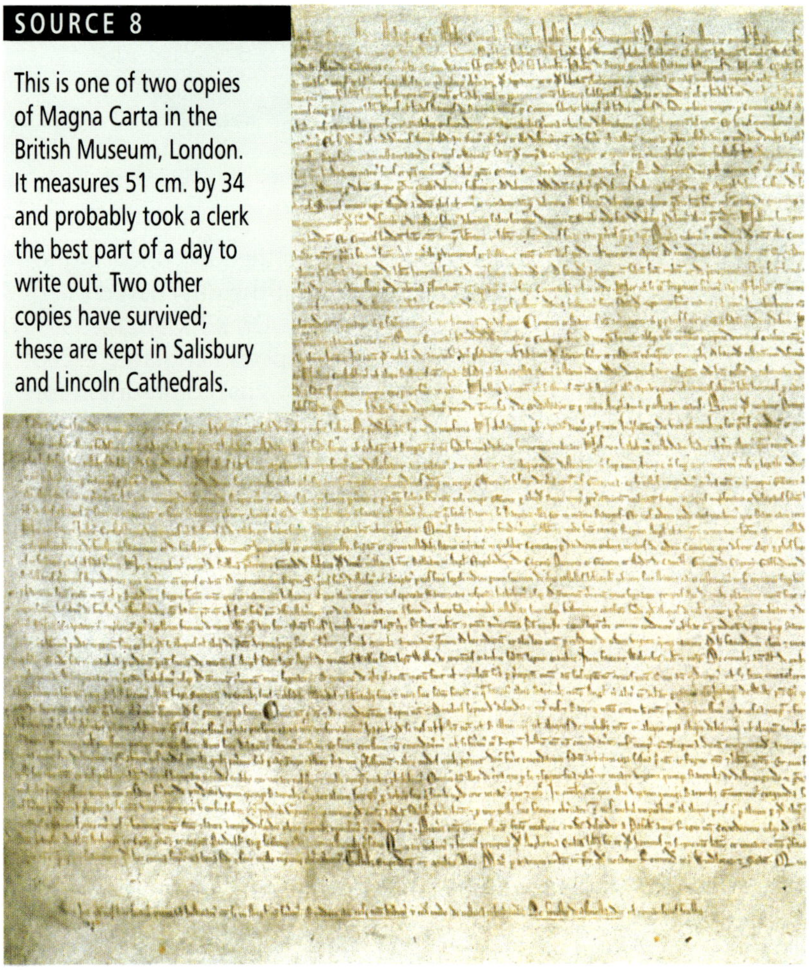

This is one of two copies of Magna Carta in the British Museum, London. It measures 51 cm. by 34 and probably took a clerk the best part of a day to write out. Two other copies have survived; these are kept in Salisbury and Lincoln Cathedrals.

thousands earlier in John's reign). The Charter said that barons must treat their knights in the same way as they wanted the King to treat them. Consequently the relief of a knight was fixed at £5 – the usual amount under Henry II.

Some of the most important parts of Magna Carta were to do with justice. John had made some barons pay him money to be sure of getting a fair trial. In future, no freeman was to be punished without a proper trial. Neither judges nor the king were to take bribes or deny justice to anyone (**Source 9**). Punishments, too, would have to be fair. For example, people were not to be fined more than they could afford to pay.

Many more baronial demands were granted in the Charter, including a reduction in the size of the royal forests. Magna Carta was frequently reissued in the years ahead and other kings besides John promised to obey its rules. People in later ages often saw rights and freedoms in the Charter which had not been intended at the time. For example, it was said that the need for the barons to agree to scutage meant that kings could not raise any kind

SOURCE 9

Here are three of the most important statements in Magna Carta. The first two gave the protection of the law to all free men. The third led, in later centuries, to the control of all taxes by Parliament. An *aid*, like a scutage or relief, was a sum of money paid to the king as the feudal lord.

No free man may be seized, imprisoned, deprived of his lands, outlawed, banished or in any way injured ... except by the lawful judgement of his equals and according to the law of the land.

To no one will we sell, deny or delay right and justice.

No scutage or aid shall be imposed in our realm except with the common counsel of the kingdom (the agreement of the barons and church leaders).

SOURCE 10

Innocent III was furious when he heard about Magna Carta. This is part of a letter he wrote to the English bishops. John had recently promised to join a Crusade to try to win back Jerusalem from the Turks.

[King John] was forced to accept an agreement which is ... illegal and unjust. The king's rights have been injured, the English nation shamed, and the whole plan for the Crusade seriously endangered. We utterly reject and condemn this settlement and ... order that the king should not dare to do what it says and the barons should not insist on it being followed. We declare the charter ... to be forever cancelled.

of tax without permission. Magna Carta helped to make future kings and governments rule more fairly and it became part of the law of the land.

Henry III and Simon de Montfort

John had no intention of keeping to the Charter. He said promises forced from him counted for nothing. As soon as he could borrow enough money to hire soldiers he went to war with the barons. Pope Innocent supported him and condemned the Charter (**Source 10**). John was still fighting when he died, suddenly, during the night of 18 October 1216, after eating and drinking too much. His nine-year-old son was crowned King Henry III and a group of barons governed the country until the boy grew up. Peace was restored and a new version of Magna Carta issued.

Henry was a gentle man with little interest in war. He loved books, painting and architecture, and spent many years rebuilding Westminster Abbey. As a king, however, he was unreliable. He raised taxes for one purpose and used them for another. He was too fond of foreign

SOURCE 11

Bronze figure of Henry III in Westminster Abbey. Henry spent a lot of money on rebuilding the Abbey and is buried there.

SOURCE 12

This part of Westminster Abbey – the south transept – was rebuilt by Henry III.

SOURCE 13

Here Matthew Paris tells a story about one of Henry III's favourites.

In the service of Geoffrey de Lusignan, the King's brother, was a certain priest, who acted as a fool and jester to the King ... and to this man the King gave the rich church of Preston ... This same priest, a Poitevin (from Poitou in France) ... we have seen pelting the King, his brother Geoffrey and other nobles, whilst walking in the orchard of St Albans, with turf, stones and green apples, and pressing the juice of unripe grapes in their eyes, like one lacking in sense ... The King of England trusts people like this to care for and protect many thousands of souls ... and rejects ... wise and proper men born in England.

favourites for the liking of his English subjects. He gave the best jobs to his French wife's friends and relatives, and appointed nearly 300 foreign clergymen to English churches (**Source 13**).

Once again, the barons felt they had a king they could not trust. They met at Oxford in 1258 and demanded that Henry should change his ways. At first, Henry agreed to their demands, but later he changed his mind and raised an army against them. In 1264 the majority of the barons, led by Simon de Montfort, Earl of Leicester, defeated the King at the battle of Lewes in Sussex.

SOURCE 14

Simon de Montfort, from a window in Chartres Cathedral, in France. Simon, a Frenchman by birth, was married to the King's sister. But this did not stop him from accusing King Henry of ruling unjustly and unfairly.

The battle of Evesham, August 1265. The map shows the movements of the armies before the battle. Gloucester and Mortimer were powerful barons who had quarrelled with Simon after being on his side at the battle of Lewes in the previous year.

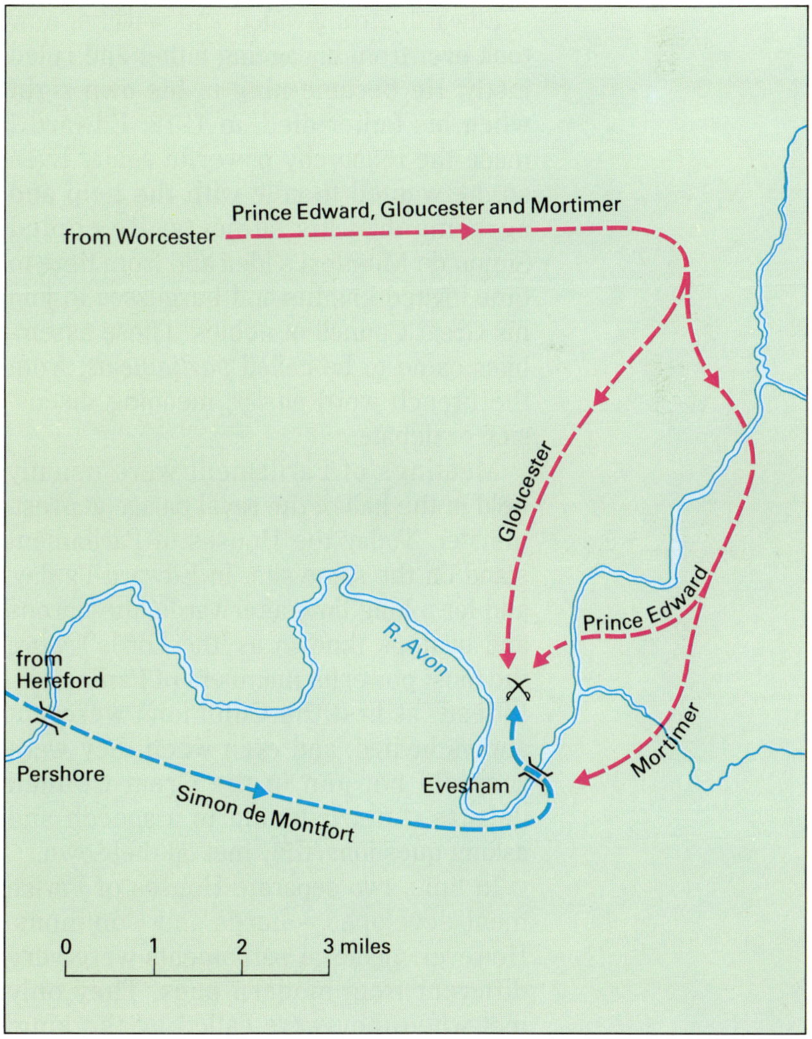

Simon de Montfort was now the real master of England. But some of the barons were jealous of his power and refused to follow him. To gain wider support, Simon held a Great Council in January 1265 to which he invited not only the nobles who supported him but also people to represent ordinary freemen. Each county was asked to elect two knights, and towns that were on his side each chose two *burgesses* (citizens).

Never before had knights and townsmen joined the barons and bishops to discuss the government of the realm. They supported Earl Simon, which is why he invited them. But the presence of 'the Commons', as they were called, was also a sign of their growing influence in England. The time was fast approaching when they would be too important to be ignored.

From Great Council to Parliament

Simon de Montfort's 'rule' came to a sudden end in August 1265. Many of his followers changed sides and rallied behind Prince Edward, the King's eldest son. Heavily outnumbered, Simon and his supporters were crushed in a bloody battle at Evesham in Worcestershire. It took only

SOURCE 15

Matthew Paris was one of those who mourned Simon de Montfort's death.

At the time of his (Simon's) death, a storm of thunder and lightning occurred, and darkness fell so that all were struck with amazement ... Thus ended the labours of that noble man Earl Simon, who gave up not only his property but also his person, to defend ... justice and the rights of the kingdom ... It is reported that Simon, after his death, was noted for working many miracles, which, however, were not made public, for fear of kings.

two hours for the royal forces to kill Simon and all the leaders of his army. Many English people were sorry he was dead (**Source 15**). They had hoped he would bring about a fairer government.

Edward, strong-willed and warlike, now took over from his ageing father and ruled justly. He became king in his own right when his father died, in 1272. Edward I made the monarchy powerful again. Even so, he wanted to rule with the help and agreement of his subjects. He copied Simon de Montfort's idea and from time to time invited knights and burgesses to join his Great Council of nobles. These assemblies came to be called *parliaments*, from the French word *parley*, meaning discussion or debate.

Meetings of Parliament were usually held in the hall of the royal palace at Westminster. Today the Houses of Parliament stand on the same site. In Edward I's day, and for a long time afterwards, the barons and bishops (known as 'the Lords') were the most powerful members of Parliament. Indeed, at first the Commons were not always invited, and even when they were they did not join in the Great Council debates. After listening to a speech and asking questions, they met on their own.

In time, two separate Houses of Parliament developed – Lords and Commons. However medieval parliaments were very different from modern ones. They only met when they were called by the king; there were no political parties and only wealthy men with property were thought fit to take part. Women had no place at all in governing the country; the same was true of ordinary villagers and tradesmen.

QUESTIONS

1. Look at Source 10. Can you explain why the Pope's attitude to John had changed so completely since the time of the Interdict?
2. In what ways does Source 13 help us to understand why there was a rebellion against Henry III?
3. How does Source 13 help to explain the views expressed by the same writer in Source 15?
4. What evidence is there in the map of the battle of Evesham that (a) Prince Edward had not expected Simon's army to cross the river, and (b) Simon made a mistake by doing so?

Petitions and taxes

Members of the Commons presented *petitions* (requests) to the king. These could be about such things as quarrels between groups of merchants, hardship caused by floods or storms, cases of injustice or a breakdown in law and order in a particular area. There were often hundreds of petitions. The king dealt only with the most important ones, leaving the rest to his officials (**Source 17**). Such petitions were the first parliamentary Bills.

If the king wanted to raise a tax, the Commons were asked to agree to it in the name of the people. Apart from this, however, the Commons did not expect to be involved in governing the country. They saw that as the king's job. Indeed, many of them seem to have had little to say in parliament (**Source 18**). In 1348, when King Edward III asked for their advice about a war in France, they replied that they were too 'ignorant and simple' to understand such matters.

SOURCE 16

Edward I and his Great Council in 1274. Llywelyn, Prince of Wales, and Alexander III, King of Scotland, were also present.

SOURCE 17

Edward I wrote to his Chancellor on 5 February 1305 to explain how he wanted the Commons' petitions dealt with.

We bid you … to make it known that all those who have petitions to bring to us and our council at our forthcoming parliament, shall bring them each day to … you and the others of our council in London [who] are to deal with as many of these petitions as you can before we come, so that the only petitions that shall come before us in person are those which cannot be dealt with without us.

Edward III (1327–77) and many kings who followed him relied heavily on taxes to pay for wars. This increased the power of the Commons and made their opinions matter. Before long they were taking important decisions. In 1382 a law from the King's Council was cancelled because the Commons did not like it. Simon de Montfort is sometimes called the founder of parliament. This is an exaggeration, but his attempt to gain more support in 1265 did change English history in ways that would have surprised him.

SOURCE 18

A poem written during the reign of Richard II (1377–99) described the way the Commons behaved when they got to Parliament. This is part of it, re-written in modern English.

Some members sat there like a nought in arithmetic, that marks a place but has no value in itself. Some had taken bribes, so that the counties they represented got no benefit from their presence … Some members slept and said little. Some stammered and mumbled and did not know what they meant to say. Some were … afraid to take any step without their masters' orders.

Assessment tasks

A *Knowledge and understanding*

1 Here are seven possible reasons why the barons rebelled against King John. If you can think of others, you may wish to add them.

- John was often cruel and he was thought to have murdered his nephew, Arthur.
- He quarrelled with the Pope and was excommunicated.
- He seemed in no hurry to end the Interdict.
- He demanded more money from the barons than previous kings had done.
- He was defeated in battle and lost most of his French lands.
- He came after a successful warrior king, Richard I.
- He denied some barons proper justice and accepted bribes from others.

Place these in what you consider to be their order of importance. Give reasons for your answer.

2 Compare the baronial rebellions faced by John and Henry III.
a In what ways were they similar?
b How were they different?

3 What were the consequences of the rebellion led by Simon de Montfort, (i) in the short term, and (ii) in the longer term?

B *Interpretations and sources*

4 Here are two contrasting opinions of King John written by historians many hundreds of years after his death.

> In his inner soul John was the worst ... of the Angevins (his family) ... He abandoned one wife and was faithless to another ... His punishments were refinements of cruelty (he perfected ways of being cruel): the starvation of children, the crushing of old men under copes (caps) of lead ... He scoffed at priests and turned his back on the mass (a church service), even amidst ... his coronation.
> (J.L. Green, 1874)

> Many of the stories about John's brutality (cruelty) were nothing but inventions. Writers repeated the worst gossip about the King as monks exchanged their news or as travellers carried it from one monastery to another. John was not a pious (religious) man, like his son, Henry III, but he certainly did not hate religion and the Church, as some writers said ... Sometimes King John was cruel, but sometimes, too, he was merciful to poor men and people in distress.
> (J.C. Holt, 1961)

a Can you explain how two historians could arrive at such different conclusions?
b Which account do you find the most convincing, and why?

5 **a** List the parts of Sources 2, 13 and 15 which suggest that the writer, Matthew Paris, was a churchman.
b What do these sources tell you about Matthew Paris himself? What kind of person do you think he was?

6 Look carefully at Source 16.
a Can you identify the people and the groups in the picture?
b What do Sources 16, 17 and 18 together tell you about medieval parliaments?
c Which of these sources do you think is the most useful to a historian, and why?

7 Neighbours at war

Relations between England, Wales and Scotland

When William I conquered England, he gave large estates on the Welsh border to the earls of Chester, Shrewsbury and Hereford. These lands were known as the Welsh marches, from the French word *marche*, meaning frontier. In return for guarding the Welsh border, these 'marcher lords' were allowed to keep any land they conquered. It was a dangerous task which could be done only by using castles as bases. The country on either side of the England-Wales border is still dotted with castles today – reminders of troubled times long ago (**Source 1**).

Wales is a land with many hills and mountains. In medieval times its people were mainly herdsmen and shepherds who wandered the hills seeking good pasture for their cattle, sheep and goats. They were hardy, warlike folk who fought and stole from each other and from the English. The songs of their *bards* (minstrels) told of quarrels, feuds and fights (**Source 2**). The marcher lords were tough fighters too – and much better equipped than the Welsh. By the thirteenth century their descendants had occupied large parts of Wales.

SOURCE 1

Ludlow Castle in Shropshire. It was built by Roger de Montgomery, the first Earl of Shrewsbury and one of William the Conqueror's most trusted barons. Roger also built a castle on the Welsh side of the border, at Montgomery – a town named after him.

SOURCE 2

This description of the Welsh was written in 1188 by Gerald of Wales, a priest who lived for a time in Henry II's household.

They make use of light weapons … the better-off go to battle mounted on horses, but most people fight on foot, because of the unevenness and marshy nature of the soil … They live neither in towns, villages nor castles, but lead a lonely life in the woods … They do not build palaces … nor lofty stone buildings, but content themselves with small huts made from the boughs of trees … Most of the land is pasture … little is cultivated.

SOURCE 3

Edward was away on a Crusade when his father died, in 1272, and he became king. Llywelyn wrote this letter to him in July 1273.

We have received the letter written in the King's name forbidding us to build a castle on our own land bear Aber Miwl, or to establish a town or market there. We are certain that this letter was not issued with your knowledge … for you know well that the rights of our principality (the part of Wales ruled by prince Llywelyn) are entirely separate from the rights of your kingdom … We and our ancestors had the power within our borders to build castles … without prohibition by anyone.

SOURCE 4

This was written in about 1307 – the year of Edward's death – by Nicholas Trevet, a chronicler who was also a friar.

Edward, king of the English … was from his earliest years devoted to soldiering. Hence the fame he won as a knight in many lands made him superior among Christian princes … His long arms … enabled him to become a swordsman second to none … and his long legs gave him his firm seat in the saddle and his mastery over the most lively thoroughbred horse.

QUESTIONS

1. Can you explain why the marcher lords had to rely so heavily upon castles?
2. Why did most Welsh people 'lead a lonely life' (Source 2) rather than live in villages or towns?
3. What do you think Llywelyn hoped to achieve by his letter (Source 3)?
4. Why do you think tenants-in-chief had to seek royal permission to do the sorts of things Llywelyn refers to in Source 3?

Llywelyn, lord of Gwynedd

Only in the north, in mountainous Gwynedd (Snowdonia), did the Welsh rule themselves. After many battles with marcher lords, the powerful chief of Gwynedd, Llywelyn ap Gruffudd, made a peace treaty with King Henry III in 1267. Llywelyn did homage to Henry as his overlord, but in the years that followed he found English rule increasingly hard to accept. When Henry's son, Edward I, became king, Llywelyn missed the coronation and refused to renew his homage (**Source 3**). Edward, a strong and experienced soldier, (**Source 4**) declared war on Llywelyn in 1277.

While marcher lords advanced through south Wales, Edward attacked in the north. Axemen cleared woodland, labourers filled ditches and carpenters built bridges across streams. By such means Edward drove thousands of soldiers and tonnes of supplies across a wilderness. The two English armies closed on Gwynedd like a pair of pincers. The pincers snapped shut when Edward's fleet captured Anglesey and cut off Llywelyn's corn supplies. Trapped and short of food, the Welsh chief was forced to give in. However, when he had done homage to Edward, he was given back Gwynedd.

The Welsh did not get on well with their English masters and frequently complained that royal officials were harsh and unjust. In 1282 Llywelyn's brother, Dafydd, led his countrymen in revolt. Llywelyn was not keen to fight Edward again, but he joined his brother. This time Edward set out to conquer the whole of Wales and showed no mercy. Dafydd and Llywelyn were surrounded in the mountains. Llywelyn escaped with a few followers but was killed by an English soldier, near Builth, in December 1282. His head was sent to London and fixed above the Tower. A few months later Dafydd was captured and executed (**Source 6**). By then Welsh resistance had already collapsed.

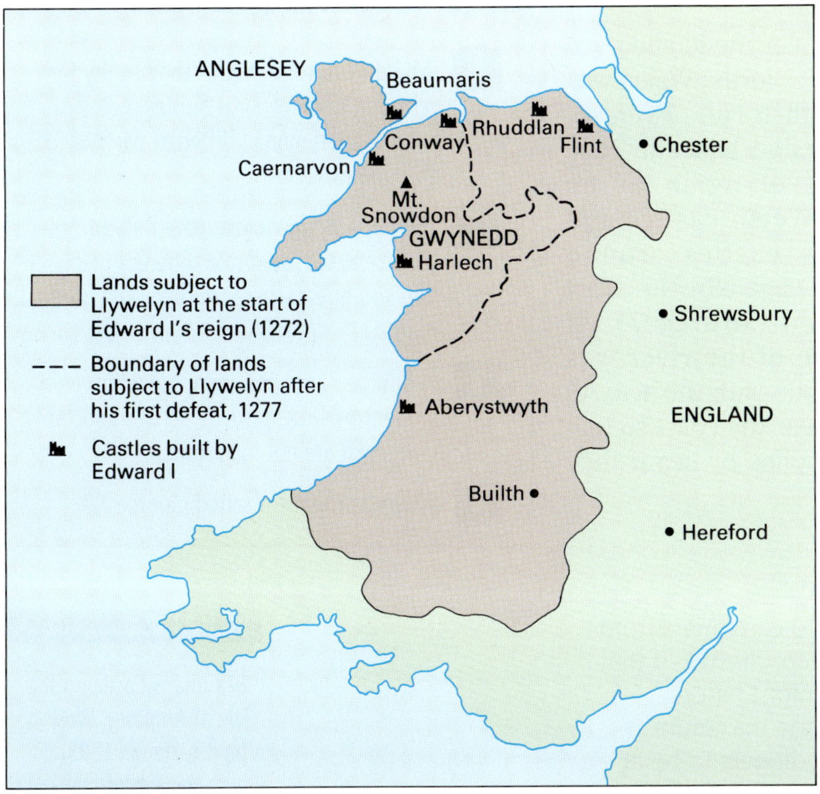

Wales in the time of Edward I

SOURCE 5

This thirteenth-century sculpture of Edward I as a boy can be seen in Westminster Abbey. When he grew up, Edward was called 'Longshanks' because he was very tall. His tomb in the Abbey was opened in 1774 and his embalmed body found to measure 1.88 metres – an enormous height for a medieval man.

SOURCE 6

Dafydd's execution, in 1283 at Shrewsbury, is described here by the monks of Lanercost, a priory close to the Scottish border.

Dafydd was first drawn (dragged along the ground by horses) as a traitor, then hanged as a thief; thirdly he was beheaded alive, and his insides burnt as a fire-raiser and murderer; fourthly his limbs were cut into four parts as the penalty for rebellion, and put on show in four … places in England – the right arm with a ring on the finger in York; the left arm in Bristol; the right leg and hip at Northampton and the left leg at Hereford.

Edwardian castles

Edward took control of Gwynedd and gave out lands to the marcher lords. Wales was now wholly under English rule. Even so, the King knew he needed bases in case the Welsh rose in revolt again. So he strengthened many Welsh castles and built a ring of new castles around Gwynedd (see map on page 69). No effort or expense was spared (**Source 7**). At Rhuddlan, the course of the river was changed to link the castle with the sea. All the new castles were near the coast so that they could receive supplies by sea if they had to face a siege.

QUESTIONS

1. Why do you think it was 'the penalty for rebellion' (Source 6) to display pieces of the executed man in different parts of the kingdom?
2. The head of the unfortunate Dafydd (Source 6) was sent to a different place. Can you guess where this was, and give a reason?
3. In Source 7, can you work out why carpenters were needed? What important craftsmen are not mentioned?
4. Why was the meat salted (Source 7)?

SOURCE 7

We can get some idea of the immense effort needed to build one of Edward's castles from this official order issued in April 1282.

Note well ... to seek 300 carpenters from the counties to be sent to Chester so that they are there by a fortnight before Whitsun. Urgent. Also the maximum number of 1000–2000 diggers to be at Chester by the same date. Carpenters and diggers to be forced to come by constables ... Also ... to ask for salt-meat from Gascony (part of France ruled by Edward).

SOURCE 8

Beaumaris Castle on the Isle of Anglesey. Work on it began in 1295, with the aim of defending towns established on the island by Edward I.

The castles Edward built round Gwynedd are some of the finest of the Middle Ages. On his travels in Europe and the Holy Land, Edward had seen improved castles with *concentric* defences (one circle of walls inside another). The living quarters were built round a central area called the *inner ward* (**Source 8**). The space between the two rings of walls formed a narrow *outer ward.* This was a deathtrap for any attackers who got over the outside wall because arrows could be fired at them from both sides.

The round towers set at intervals in the walls of these castles were important for defence. In the old square keeps, when archers shot at attackers close underneath the walls they exposed themselves to returning fire. But towers curving outwards made it easy for defenders inside to shoot along the faces of the walls. The clever design of Edward's castles can still be seen today because many have survived in good repair. At one of them, Caernarvon, Edward's son, the future Edward II, was proclaimed 'Prince of Wales' in 1301 – a title still given to the monarch's eldest son.

SOURCE 9

Caernarvon Castle and the town that has grown up around it. The castle's towers and walls were copied from the city of Constantinople.

Owain Glyndwr's revolt

Edwardian castles helped later medieval kings to keep a firm hold on Wales. Yet they did not prove unconquerable. Two of the strongest, Harlech and Aberystwyth, were captured during the last great Welsh rising. This was led by Owain Glyndwr, a well-to-do landowner, lawyer and soldier. In 1400 he claimed he was the man chosen by God to free Wales from the English. Many discontented Welshmen joined him, complaining about English laws and taxes.

The rebels began by burning the town of Ruthin and attacking its castle. This was held by a marcher lord, Grey of Ruthin, a bitter enemy of Glyndwr. The English King, Henry IV, did not take the revolt seriously at first. In any case, he had plenty of troubles of his own from powerful nobles at home. Soon Glyndwr's revolt was spreading, first to the towns in the north and then across most of Wales (**Source 10**). By 1404 he was behaving like a king. He called Welsh parliaments, made an alliance with the King of France and planned to set up a separate Welsh Church.

SOURCE 10

Owain Glyndwr's rebellion is recorded in the chronicles of Adam of Usk (1352–1430), a priest and lawyer. These events occurred in 1402.

On the day of St Alban (22 June), near Knighton in Wales, there was a hard fought battle between the English ... and the Welsh, with a terrible killing of about 8000 souls. Owain won the victory ... With a following of 30,000 men ... Owain captured castles ... and set fire to towns ... In this year the King, with more than 100,000 men divided into three armies, invaded Wales to make war on Owain. But he (Owain) and his poor wretches stayed in their caves and woods. So the King burned and plundered the land and went home with countless stolen cattle.

Then the English hit back. Henry IV's son, the future Henry V, was an outstanding soldier. He took charge of the royal forces and began to drive the rebels from the castles and towns they had captured. Harlech and Aberystwyth were won back in 1408–9 and after that the rebellion fizzled out. Glyndwr became a hunted man. In 1413 he went into hiding and no one knows when or where he died. The English Parliament passed harsh laws against the Welsh. They were barred from official jobs and in some cases not allowed to own land. But they managed to keep alive their language and customs, which have survived to the present day.

The puppet king of Scotland

Scotland had its own line of kings from earliest times. The country they ruled fell into two halves. In the Lowlands, south of the Firth of Forth, many families were descended from the English and Normans. Here the way of life was similar to that in England. The Highlanders of the north, however, were much more like the wandering herdsmen of Wales. They disliked the English and even looked upon Scottish Lowlanders as foreigners.

At the start of Edward I's reign, the Scots were ruled by a strong and popular monarch, Alexander III. But in March 1286 disaster struck when Alexander was thrown from his horse and killed. He did not have any sons and his daughter, who had married the King of Norway, was dead. She left a baby girl, Margaret, who was then three years old. The 'Maid of Norway', as she was called, was proclaimed queen of Scotland. But four years later she was taken ill while sailing from Norway and died in the Orkney Islands.

Thirteen Scottish nobles claimed the vacant throne. To avoid civil war between their supporters, Edward I was invited to

SOURCE 11

Like a king, Owain Glyndwr used a great seal. Its two sides are shown here.

Scotland in the time of Edward I

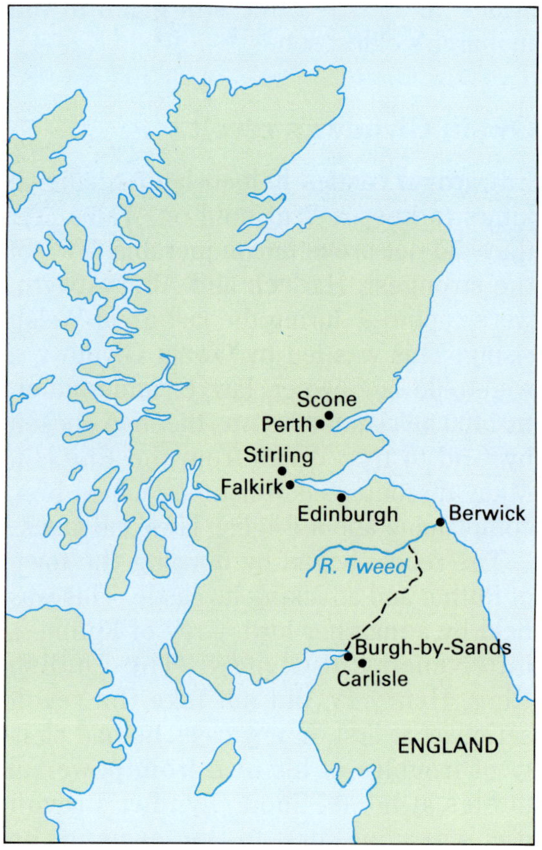

decide who should be king (**Source 12**). This gave him a chance to interfere in Scotland's affairs. In 1292 he chose John Balliol, Lord of Galloway. It was a fair decision, but the English King made Balliol do homage and accept him as overlord. Many Scots now looked upon Balliol as a 'puppet king' controlled by Edward (**Source 13**). When Balliol eventually decided to stand up to the English King, Edward marched a powerful army into Scotland and overthrew him.

Wallace and Bruce

Edward now controlled Scotland. He wanted the Scots to believe that they would never have a king of their own again. So he went to Scone Abbey, near Perth, and carried away to England the block of stone on which Scottish kings had been

SOURCE 12

A small group of nobles had been appointed to rule Scotland on behalf of the Maid of Norway. After her death , one of them, the Bishop of St Andrews,wrote to Edward I as follows.

The kingdom is disturbed and the people distressed. Sir Robert Bruce came with many followers, but as yet we do not know what he intends to do. The earls of Mar and Atholl are already collecting their army; and some other nobles of the land are won over to their party, and because of this there is fear of general war and a great slaughter of men unless Your Majesty finds a speedy remedy.

SOURCE 13

A later drawing of John Balliol. What point is the artist trying to make, and how does he get it across?

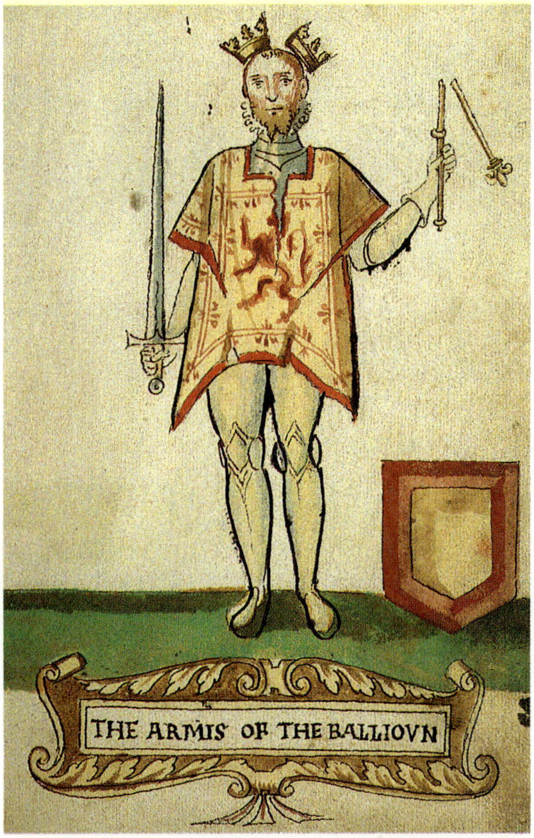

SOURCE 14

The coronation chair in Westminster Abbey. It was made for Edward I so that he could enclose under the seat the Stone of Scone, after taking it from the Scots. Since 1308, every English monarch except Edward V and Edward VIII has been crowned on this chair.

crowned. Many Scottish noblemen did not mind the English ruling them. Some had land on both sides of the border; others already served the king as officials in castles or towns. But the ordinary farmers and clansmen of Scotland would not accept English rule without a fight. Led by a humble knight, William Wallace, they rebelled and beat the English at Stirling in September 1297.

Next spring, Edward led a large army north to teach the Scots a lesson. He knew that the English troops at Stirling had been beaten by disciplined ranks of Scots with long spears. Edward's answer to such tactics was to take thousands of archers armed with longbows. These deadly weapons, up to 2 metres high, were made of yew, ash or elm. Their iron-tipped arrows travelled with such force that they could pass through a man's leg and pin him to his saddle (**Source 15**).

When the two armies met, at Falkirk, in 1298, Edward's archers let loose a deadly hail of arrows upon the masses of spearmen. Then his horsemen poured through the gaps left by the dead and dying, breaking the Scottish ranks. Wallace fled into hiding. For seven years he was a hunted outlaw until he was finally captured, taken to London and cruelly executed.

Edward spent his last years sending armies to Scotland to capture castles, destroy towns and kill all who dared to defy him. He was nicknamed 'the Hammer of the Scots' because he treated them so badly. Yet still the Scots fought back. In 1306, Robert Bruce, grandson of one of the nobles who had earlier claimed the throne, was crowned king of Scotland. It seemed an empty title. Bruce had few followers at first and lived the life of an outlaw. Edward was soon on his way north to crush him. But the English King, now old and feeble, died in July 1307 at Burgh-by-Sands, near Carlisle.

The battle of Bannockburn

The dying King had begged his son, now Edward II, to carry his bones before the army until Scotland was conquered. Instead, the young King returned to England and buried his father in Westminster Abbey. Bruce, meanwhile, was getting stronger. Year by year more men joined him, as he launched daring raids on English strongholds. Castle after castle fell into Scottish hands until, in 1313, Stirling, the greatest of them all, was seriously threatened. Its governor said he would surrender the castle if he was not relieved by the English King within a year.

Edward II could not give up Stirling without a fight. In June 1314 he entered Scotland with 20,000 men – a huge army for those days (**Source 17**). Bruce, outnumbered by at least three to one, faced him on a wooded ridge alongside a stream called the Bannockburn, south of Stirling. The Scottish King knew he would have to

SOURCE 15

Using a longbow required skill and plenty of practice. Medieval kings often urged their subjects to practise archery, as in this order from Edward III to the Lord-lieutenant of Kent in 1363.

We ... hereby order that in all places in your county ... it shall be proclaimed that every man, if he is able-bodied, shall upon holidays make use, in his games, of bows and arrows ... and so learn and practise archery. Moreover we order that you prohibit under penalty of imprisonment ... stone, wood and iron throwing; handball, football or hockey ... cock-fighting, or other such idle games.

QUESTIONS

1. Inviting Edward to help solve Scottish problems (Source 12) was risky. Why did the Scots do it?
2. Why is John Balliol (Source 13) shown with his sceptre, crown and coat cut in two?
3. Why did the English put the 'Stone of Scone' in their coronation chair (Source 14)?
4. What was Edward III's reason for describing most games as 'idle' (Source 15)?

SOURCE 16

Stirling Castle today – rising high above the town. Very few of its medieval buildings remain.

SOURCE 17

The advance of Edward II's army into Scotland in 1314 is described here by an unknown author writing at the end of Edward's reign.

There were in that company quite enough [soldiers] to invade the whole of Scotland ... The King therefore took confidence and courage from such a great and impressive force and hurried day by day to the appointed place ... Brief were the halts for sleep, briefer still for food; hence horses, horsemen and foot-soldiers were worn out with toil and hunger, and if they did not do well it was hardly their fault.

SOURCE 18

This picture of Edward II (1307–27) and his queen, Isabella, comes from a book written in 1326. It was not a happy marriage and in the end they grew to hate each other. Edward was not a soldier king like his father and the defeat at Bannockburn made him very unpopular. He was finally overthrown by his barons and cruelly murdered at Berkeley Castle in Gloucestershire.

SOURCE 19

The Franciscan friar who wrote this account of Bannockburn based it upon the report of an eyewitness.

When the armies met, and the great horses of the English charged the spears of the Scots, as though into a dense forest, there arose a great and terrible crash of spears broken and of horses wounded to the death ... Now the English in the rear could not reach the Scots because the leading division was in the way ... the only thing they could do was escape ... Many nobles and others fell into [the Bannockburn] with their horses in the crush ... and many were never able to get out of the ditch.

SOURCE 20

Here is part of the famous 'Declaration of Arbroath' (1320). It took the form of a letter to the Pope, who had been on the side of the English in their war with the Scots.

If he (Robert Bruce) should give up what he has begun, and agree to make us or our kingdom subject to the King of England or the English, we should at once drive him out as an enemy ... and make some other man our king. For as long as one hundred men shall remain alive, we shall never under any conditions accept the domination of the English. It is not for glory, nor riches, nor honours that we are fighting but for freedom alone, which no worthy man will give up except with his life.

SOURCE 21

Statue of Robert Bruce on the site of the battle of Bannockburn. Much of the battlefield is now occupied by a housing estate.

deal with thousands of horsemen so he chose marshy ground and got his troops to dig pits and cover them up with brushwood.

The battle began, on 24 June, with Scottish spearmen attacking downhill. In the fierce fighting that followed, the size of the English army proved a disadvantage as they crowded and jostled each other. Horses and men fell into a tangle of dead and dying. Watching from a hillside were the Scottish camp followers – women, children and old men who travelled with the army. They saw the English were in trouble and ran down the hill, cheering and waving poles. The English, thinking it was another army coming to attack them, turned and fled (**Source 19**). King Edward left behind a fortune in money and jewels. He also left thousands of his men dead on the battlefield.

Bannockburn made sure that Scotland remained a free country. In 1320 Scottish nobles gathered at Arbroath Abbey and issued a Declaration of Independence (**Source 20**). Eight years later, a new English king, Edward III, finally made peace with Bruce and accepted him as King of Scotland. It was a further 300 years before the two crowns were united: James VI of Scotland became James I of England in 1603 after Elizabeth I died childless. In the meantime, the two countries went on quarrelling and fighting.

Assessment tasks

A *Knowledge and understanding*

1 In 1291 the Scottish lords asked Edward I to decide who should be king of Scotland. Less than thirty years later, in the Declaration of Arbroath, the Scots stated their determination to resist English interference. What events between these two dates changed their attitude towards the English?

2 a Why do you think Edward I wanted to unite Wales and Scotland with England?

b What are the advantages and disadvantages of such a union from the point of view of each country concerned?

c Find out what you can about the attitudes of the Welsh and Scots today to the union with England.

3 In medieval times, why were the English more successful in conquering Wales than Scotland? Among many possible factors, you should consider the following:

- the size of the two countries
- their distance from the centre of England
- the nature of the land to be conquered
- their leaders and armies.

Which do you judge to be the most important.

B Interpretations and sources

4 Was it Llywelyn's fault that Edward I attacked him in 1277, or was the King chiefly responsible for the war? Here are the views of two historians.

> Edward was away crusading; but from the moment that he came back to England matters between him and the Prince of Wales (Llywelyn) went badly ... Llywelyn ... distrusted the new King and when Edward I was crowned with great splendour in London he refused to be present. Nor would he ... swear fealty (do homage) to him. His father's long imprisonment in the Tower was a warning of what might befall himself if he ventured out of Wales to do homage to a King who was plainly no friend of his.
> (Elizabeth Inglis-Jones, 1955)

> The government of England [was] in favour of peace ... both during Edward's absence and after his return ... Chance after chance had been given to the prince (Llywelyn) to appear to pay the homage ... [But] Llywelyn evidently intended to prolong the unrest ... His object was simply to strengthen Wales, to profit by Edward's absence, and to defy invasion by getting ready beforehand.
> (John E. Morris, 1901)

a On what points do these accounts disagree?

b Are the disagreements based on fact or opinion, or both?

c Who do *you* think was mainly responsible for the war, and why?

5 Look again at Sources 4, 6, 10 and 17. For each, can you work out whether it is written from an English, Welsh or Scottish point of view? Give reasons for your answer.

6 Which parts of Source 19 suggest that:

a Bruce had chosen the ground to suit his own soldiers?

b the English might have done better with different tactics and weapons?

c the writer used the memories of someone who was at the battle?

8 Craftsmen and Merchants

Town life and trade

SOURCE 1

This plan of Canterbury dates from the sixteenth century; but it is unlikely that the town had changed much since medieval times. Can you find the cathedral? Notice that, as the town has grown, houses and churches have been built outside the walls.

Look at the plan of Canterbury (**Source 1**). Unlike towns today, it is surrounded by a high stone wall with gates. Most medieval towns had walls or earth banks to keep out robbers and tramps. Towns were centres of trade – places to which people came with money and valuable goods. Traders needed all the protection they could get, especially as there were no police in those days. So the gates were guarded at night and all visitors questioned (**Source 2**).

Another difference between medieval Canterbury and modern towns is its size. Most medieval towns were no bigger than large villages today. Historians estimate that only five towns – London, York, Bristol, Coventry and Norwich – had well over 1,000 houses at the start of the fifteenth century. Of these, London was by far the biggest with about 40,000 people. Yet even in London town-dwellers were never far from the sights and sounds of the countryside (**Source 3**). Open fields outside the

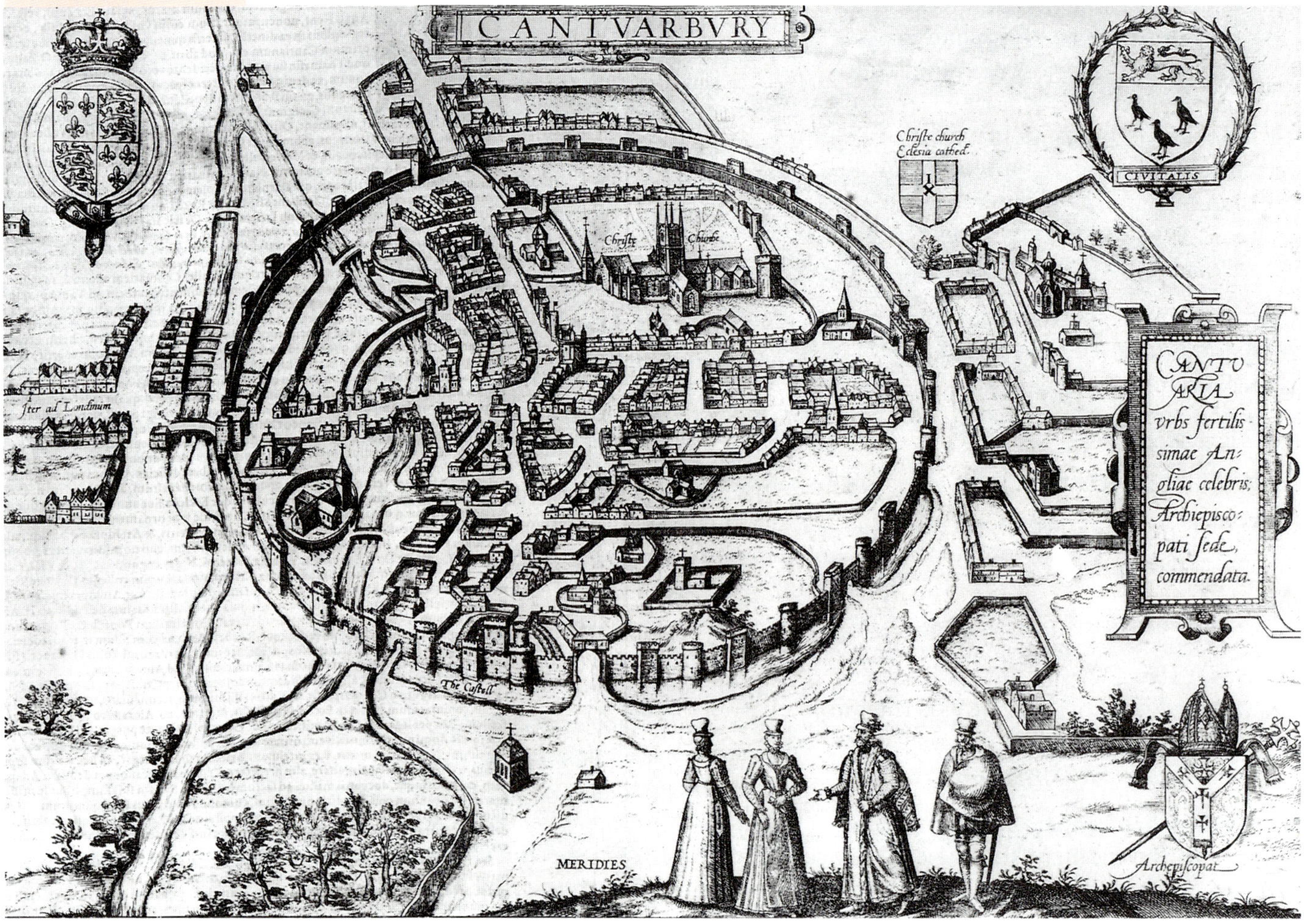

walls supplied much of their food, pigs wandered in the streets and cattle were brought inside the gates at nightfall.

Streetlife

Most town streets were narrow. A few might be laid with cobble stones; the rest were just trodden-down earth. Houses were mostly built of timber with white plaster walls. They often had a workshop on the ground floor with wooden shutters opening on to the street. Passers-by could see articles being made inside and order what they needed. The craftsman and his family usually lived upstairs, over the shop. Elsewhere, on market day, goods were displayed on stalls and benches in the streets. Every town had its weekly market when people came in from the local villages.

Towns had no drains or sewers and no one to collect rubbish. People dumped garbage in the streets and emptied chamber pots and buckets out of their windows. An open channel running down the middle of the street carried sewage and slops to the nearest river. The same river often provided much of the town's drinking water, so it is not surprising that diseases spread rapidly (**Source 6**).

QUESTIONS

1. Canterbury grew in size and importance after 1170. Can you think of a reason for this?
2. How does the population of your town, or the town nearest to you, compare with that of medieval London?
3. In what ways would York's Shambles (Source 4) have looked different in the Middle Ages from the way it is pictured here?
4. In medieval towns, people of the same trade were often found along one street. Look up the meaning of the word shambles to find out the trade carried on in the street of that name.

SOURCE 2

This royal order for the safety of town-dwellers was issued during the reign of Edward I, in 1285.

The King has commanded that in the great towns, which are enclosed, the gates be shut from sunset until sunrise ... And it is commanded that watches be kept, as has been usual in time past ... in every city by six men at every gate ... And if any stranger pass by them, he shall be arrested until morning, and if no suspicion be found, he shall be released; and if they find cause of suspicion, he shall be delivered to the sheriff.

SOURCE 3

We can see the importance of the countryside to town-dwellers in this twelfth-century account of London life. It was written by William fitz Stephen, one of Henry II's justices.

The city's farmland ... produces plentiful crops ... Also in the northern outskirts of London are excellent wells, with sweet, clear drinking water ... These are visited by crowds ... looking for fresh air on summer evenings ... Outside one of the gates is a field [Smithfield] ... where, every sixth day of the week, there is a well-attended show of fine horses for sale ... Many of the citizens delight themselves [by hunting] with hawks and hounds.

SOURCE 4

The Shambles in York. This still has the appearance of a medieval street, with the upper storeys of some houses overhanging the shops below.

SOURCE 5

Stalls in a medieval market. Notice the cobbled street. Can you work out what these traders are selling?

SOURCE 6

Complaints from Edward I's ministers about the state of the town of York led to this royal order in 1298.

The air [of York] is so corrupted and infected by the pig-sties situated in the King's highways ... and by the pigs feeding and frequently wandering about in the streets and lanes, and by dung and dunghills and many other foul things placed in the streets, that great disgust overtakes the King's ministers staying in that town.... The King ... orders the bailiffs ... to have the pig-sties pulled down and removed without delay and the streets and lanes cleaned.

SOURCE 7

To reduce the risk of fire, the city of London made these building regulations in 1189.

Whoever wishes to build, let him take care, if he loves himself and his goods, that he does not make the roof of reeds or rushes ... but only of tile ... When two neighbours agree to build between themselves a wall of stone, each shall give a foot and a half (half a metre) of land ... The council of citizens ... advises that all ale-houses be forbidden ... except those belonging to persons willing to build of stone ... They say also that there should be a tub full of water before every house.

After dark, there were new dangers to add to the dirt and disease. Thieves and murderers lurked in the unlit streets, especially in London and the larger towns. The risk of attack was so great that a *curfew* (warning bell) was rung at sunset to tell the taverns, or ale-houses, to close and all citizens to go home. In some towns, tavern-keepers who failed to close on time were fined.

Fire was another hazard in medieval towns. Flames spread quickly among closely-packed wooden buildings. To check fires, people pulled down houses in the path of the flames with ropes and long fire-hooks (**Source 7**). The best safeguard against fire was to build houses of stone, spaced out with gardens. But only nobles and rich merchants could afford to do this. The finest stone houses in towns had tiled floors and roofs, brick fireplaces and glass windows ahead of most country manor houses.

SOURCE 8

This drawing in the bottom margin of a medieval book shows part of London in the fourteenth century. It reminds us that medieval towns had many churches. There were well over 100 in London by the end of the Middle Ages, and Norwich had fifty.

SOURCE 9

As guilds grew rich and powerful, they built themselves fine guildhalls like this one at Lavenham in Suffolk. The guildhall was often rented to the town council for its meetings.

Town charters and guilds

Some towns began as market-places. Others grew up at a good harbour, by a shallow river-crossing or round a castle. Towns were on land either ruled directly by the king or held by one of his tenants. Town-dwellers therefore owed services to their lord, in the same way as village peasants (see Chapter 4). But most of them wanted to spend all their time making and selling goods. So they bargained with the king or lord to let them give up labour services and pay money instead. The details of such agreements were set out in a charter.

A town with a charter gained the title of borough. Its citizens were no longer villeins. They paid rent for the land (*burgage*) they lived on and were called *burgesses*. Most towns obtained a charter from the king allowing them to have their own local council. They could elect a mayor and aldermen ('elder men') and set up their own law court. Royal charters also allowed craftsmen and traders to form an association called a merchant guild.

Merchant guilds encouraged trade. They also controlled it for the benefit of their members. They made merchants from elsewhere pay *tolls* (taxes) on goods they sold in the town. The guild also paid out money to members who were sick, old or in trouble. London did not have a merchant guild. Instead, each group of craftsmen – carpenters, shoemakers, brewers, goldsmiths and many more – formed separate *craft* guilds. Craft guilds appeared in other towns by the fourteenth century. Each had strict rules controlling the quality and price of goods. Anyone found breaking them was punished **(Sources 10 and 11)**.

Craft guilds were run by master-craftsmen – those with their own workshops who employed others to work for them. This makes guilds different from modern trade unions, which do not normally include employers. The guild masters set the standards of workmanship. They also trained new recruits, called *apprentices*. An apprentice lived in his master's house and agreed to work, unpaid, for a fixed number of years (**Source 12**).

After serving his apprenticeship, a young man was paid by the day as a *journeyman* (the French *journée* means a day). A journeyman was free to work for any master, in any town. To become a master himself, he had to prove his skill to guild officials by making a 'masterpiece' of his work. Even if he passed this test, he might not be able to afford to set up his own workshop. Some craftsmen remained journeymen all their lives.

Guilds were important to towns in many ways. The richer ones founded chapels, schools and *almshouses* (homes for poor or elderly members). Craft guilds also organised many of the town's entertainments. 'Miracle plays', in which guild members acted Bible stories, in English, were espe-

SOURCE 10 and 11

City of London records tell us what happened to traders who tried to cheat customers. The first occurred in 1364; the second in 1387.

10 The four supervisors of the sale of wines … said that John Penrose was guilty of the sale of … unsound and unwholesome … red wine … so cheating the common people … [It was ordered] that John Penrose shall drink a draught of the same wine which he sold to the common people; and the remainder of the wine shall then be poured on the head of John Penrose; and he shall give up trading as a wineseller in the City of London for ever.

11 Robert Porter, servant of John Gibbe, baker of Stratford, was brought here, into the Guildhall of London, before Nicholas Extone, Mayor … and questioned, for when the same Mayor on that day went into Chepe, to test the bread … Robert, knowing that the bread of his master, in a certain cart, was not of full weight, took a penny loaf, and in it … inserted a piece of iron … And for this falsity and deceit, it was judged that he should be taken from there to Cornhill and put on the pillory … for one hour, with the loaf and piece of iron hung round his neck.

SOURCE 12

This is part of the agreement made in Preston, Lancashire, between a master *mercer* (a dealer in expensive cloths such as silk) and his apprentice, in 1393.

John Adamson of Foxton will serve … John de Walton in pure apprenticeship for the term of six years … John de Walton shall instruct and inform John Adamson in his art and shall let him out reasonably and keep him in food and clothing, in shoes and all other necessary things … And John Adamson … shall not leave doors or windows of his master open at night … and he shall not take a wife without his master's consent … And during the sixth year John de Walton shall pay to John Adamson ten shillings of silver … as his pay for that year.

QUESTIONS

1. Why might two neighbours want to 'build between themselves a wall of stone' (Source 7)?
2. What was a pillory (Source 11)? What happened when a wrongdoer was put on one?
3. Why do you think the apprentice John Adamson (Source 12) was not allowed to get married without his master's consent?
4. Can you think of a reason why John Adamson (Source 12) was paid during the last year of his apprenticeship?

SOURCE 13

A recent performance of a miracle play, in Oxfordshire, by actors dressed in fifteenth-century costume. Plays were not performed in theatres with fixed stages until the time of Shakespeare, at the end of the sixteenth century.

SOURCE 14

The choir (east end) of Gloucester Cathedral. It was built in the years 1337–50 by master-mason William of Ramsey. This style was followed for the rest of the Middle Ages. Look up the meaning of the word perpendicular. Why do you think this is called the perpendicular style of architecture? The way the stone is cut makes it seem a lighter material than it really is. Compare this picture with that of the Norman church on page 24.

cially popular in the fifteenth century. The stage was a large decorated wagon called a *pageant* which was drawn around the town. A lot of effort went into the scenery. The Mouth of Hell was made to open and shut, angels rose to heaven on ladders, and one guild hired a shipwright to build Noah's ark.

The stonemason's craft

Most things made in the Middle Ages, including wooden buildings, rotted away long ago. But the work of the stonemason lives on. Nearly all the cathedrals and big churches in Britain today are medieval buildings, repaired and enlarged over many centuries. Building in stone was so expensive that only the rich could afford it. The Church, with its rents, tithes and many generous gifts, was the richest of all.

Every town had its carpenters, tilers, plasterers and other building tradesmen. But masons usually had to be brought in from outside. Masons had a hard life, travelling from job to job. They worked long hours, especially in the extra daylight of summer, and were not paid when frost, snow or storms held up work (**Source 15**). Their cutting tools, though tipped with steel, were easily blunted and often in need of sharpening with files or grindstones. Accidents were common, usually as a result of falling from scaffolding or being hit by stones lifted on ropes and pulleys.

Masons found it difficult to belong to a local guild because they travelled around. Instead, they formed 'lodges' on each building site. Leaders of the lodge settled the pay and working conditions with whoever was employing them. A master-mason was usually appointed to design the building and supervise the work. Although this was a very important job, the wages of most master-masons were not much higher than those of the journeymen.

SOURCE 15

Here are some of the conditions that had to be followed by masons and others working on York cathedral in about 1352.

Masons, carpenters and other workmen ought to begin to work ... at sunrise and ... they shall continue to work as long as they can see by daylight. Also each mason shall take one day's wage less for the week in winter, that is from Michaelmas (29 September) to Easter, than in summer. Also when two feast days (holidays) happen in one week, each loses one day's wage and when three occur, half that week.

Local stone was used for building wherever possible, to reduce transport costs. Bricks, baked from local clay, were used increasingly after the twelfth century. These were easier and cheaper to carry. The Romans had built in brick, but then the craft died out in Britain for 700–800 years. It was rediscovered by English travellers in Europe. Another craft learned from the Continent was window-glazing, especially with stained glass. By the thirteenth century, nearly all churches and other important buildings in England had glass windows.

Wool and cloth

Many fine buildings in medieval England were paid for out of profits from the wool trade. English wool was the best in Europe and the main source of the country's wealth. Every year merchants sold thousands of sacks to Flanders (now Belgium) and northern Italy – the main centres of cloth-making in Europe. At the ports, the king's customs officers collected taxes on every shipment of wool. This was one of the main ways in which kings paid for their armies.

The English did well out of their wool. But they realised they would do even better by making it into cloth themselves. Some woollen cloth had been made in England for centuries, but it was not of the

SOURCE 16

This thirteenth-century illustration shows a king discussing a building scheme – probably with the master-mason and the carpenter of the works.

best quality. Kings tried to encourage improvements in the home industry (**Source 18**). But the main encouragement to English cloth-makers was the hope of getting a share in Europe's richest trade. The urge to make profits led merchant 'clothiers' to organise cloth-workers more efficiently.

The clothier bought a large amount of wool and had it spun into yarn. This was usually done by young women and girls, which explains the term 'spinster' for an unmarried woman. He then had the yarn made into cloth by putting it out to groups of craftsmen working at home. These included weavers, dyers and *fullers*, who beat the cloth in water to shrink and thicken it. Such craftsmen were often scattered around several villages or small towns. They were paid wages by the clothier who then sold the finished product himself.

Woollen cloth-making first grew rapidly in East Anglia, at places such as Norwich and Colchester. Later the Cotswold Hills of Somerset and Gloucestershire became the main centre of the industry. One reason for this was the growing use of fulling-mills – water-wheels which turned wooden hammers to beat the cloth. These required fast-running streams of the kind that flowed only in hilly areas. By the fifteenth century, cloth from Cotswold villages such as Castle Combe, Stroud and Bradford-on-Avon was fetching top prices at home and abroad. English cloth-makers were already drawing ahead of their Continental rivals.

QUESTIONS

1. Why were stonemasons paid less in the winter than in the summer (Source 15)? Do you think this was fair?
2. Can you describe what each of the builders pictured in Source 16 is doing? What tools can you see?
3. Why do you think Edward III needed to give his 'special protection and defence' (Source 18) to the cloth workers from Flanders?
4. How many common surnames can you think of that go back to the medieval building and woollen cloth trades?

SOURCE 17

This sofa-like object is in the House of Lords at Westminster. It is stuffed with English wool and the Lord Chancellor, who chairs the debates, sits on it. The custom of sitting on the Woolsack, as it is called, goes back to the Middle Ages. It is a reminder that England's wealth was once based on wool.

SOURCE 18

Edward III invited cloth workers from Flanders to settle in England and pass on their skills to English workers. This 'letter of protection' was written in 1331.

John Kempe of Flanders, weaver of woollen cloths, will come to stay within our realm of England to practise his craft, and to instruct and teach those here wishing to learn … We have taken John and his men, servants and apprentices … into our special protection and defence … We are obliged to make similar letters of protection for other men of that craft,. and for dyers and fullers wishing to come from foreign parts to stay within our realm.

SOURCE 19

This fifteenth-century French picture shows 'spinsters' at work. The woman on the left is spinning. She has a *distaff* under her arm (a stick with prongs to hold the wool) and is drawing out and twisting the yarn with a *spindle* (like a heavy spinning top). Next to her, the woman holding things that look like hair brushes is 'carding' or disentangling the wool to prepare it for spinning. Above, a lady weaves cloth on a loom.

SOURCE 20

A group of well-to-do women pictured in the fifteenth century. Notice their style of dress. The wives of wealthy merchants and landowners took charge of the household and also often played an important part in the family's business affairs. They kept accounts, hired workers, arranged the marriages of their children and took all sorts of other decisions whenever their husbands were away from home.

Trade by land and sea

As well as the weekly market, some larger towns held a fair each year. Usually for a week, local traders were joined by merchants from distant parts, some even from abroad. The well-to-do bought goods that were not always easy to get, including weapons, leather saddles, fine silks and perfumes. Poorer folk were more interested in merry-making than trading. There were jugglers, acrobats, dancing bears and often wrestling matches too. People got drunk in the taverns and many crimes were committed (**Source 21**). Some traditional fairs carry on today, but now they are purely for amusement.

Most merchants carried their goods to fairs and markets on packhorses. Carts held more, but often they could not be used because roads were so full of holes and ruts. No proper roads had been built in Britain since the Romans left, in about AD 400. Where possible, goods were carried long distances on river barges or by sea. But even sea trade had its difficulties. Ships were often unsafe in bad weather and pirates a danger along many coasts.

Overseas trade with Europe was controlled by powerful groups of foreign merchants. The largest of these was the *Hanseatic League*, an alliance of north German cities (*hanse* means a company of merchants). The League gained special privileges for its members, such as reduced port taxes. Its ships brought timber, furs, salted herrings and iron to London and the east coast ports of England. They returned with wool or cloth, lead, tin, corn and hides for sale in Europe.

The Hanseatic League traded mainly in northern Europe. Trade with the Mediterranean lands was mostly carried by Italian ships from cities such as Venice and Genoa. They brought rare luxury goods from the East – silks, Persian carpets, jewels and glassware. Among their most prized goods were spices, including pepper, ginger, nutmeg and cloves, which greatly improved the taste of food in well-to-do homes. Italian merchants, skilled at

SOURCE 21

At fairs, special courts were held to deal with such things as cheating, theft and assault. They were called Piepowder Courts because the French *piepoudreux* (dusty feet) was a word for hawkers, who go from place to place selling goods. The following cases are from the records of St Ives Fair in Huntingdonshire.

AD 1291 John, son of William, son of Agnes of Lynn, who is ten years of age, was found … stealing a purse during the fair; but because he is not old enough [to be punished] … it is ordered that he be banished from St Ives and the fair.

AD 1300 Ives Vickery [and five others] who were appointed to watch in Cross Lane near the canvas booth … watched badly, so that the canvas booth was broken into by robbers, and the greater part of the canvas and other goods were taken. Therefore … they are fined 3 shillings.

SOURCE 22

Packhorses carrying wool. In open country, merchants often travelled in groups – or 'packhorse trains' – to give each other some protection against robbers.

SOURCE 23

Model of a fifteenth-century *cog*. Ships like this carried cargoes all over northern Europe. Some had more than one mast, but their square sails still made progress against the wind difficult. Such ships were unsafe in stormy weather. However the magnetic compass (a Chinese invention) made navigation more reliable in the later Middle Ages. In wartime, cogs were used for fighting. This explains the 'castles' at each end, which were used by archers. We still call a raised deck at the front of a ship the *fo'c'sle* (forecastle).

SOURCE 24

The following complaints were made by English merchants against the Hanseatic League in 1440.

We hear repeatedly ... complaints of the merchants of our realm ... about the injuries and hurts done to them ... The governors of the town of Danzig make English merchants pay unfair taxes ... [Yet when these] are paid, many of the ships of the same merchants, prepared and ready to sail, are not allowed to leave ... Also, Thomas Chapman, a citizen of York, John Forster of Hull, John Hereford of Newcastle and other subjects of the king ... entirely innocent, were taken in the tcwn of Danzig ... with their hands tied ... before the judge there and, by fear of death, were made to pay heavy and burdensome sums of money.

banking, became the richest in London. But Londoners grew jealous of their wealth. From time to time there were riots against foreign traders and some were killed.

For centuries, most of England's overseas trade was carried in foreign ships. But gradually English shipping took a greater share. Groups of *Merchant Adventurers* were formed in the main English ports. They aimed to establish trading centres abroad, just as foreign merchants had done in England, and sell more English goods. Such moves were unpopular in foreign ports and English seamen were often ill-treated (**Source 24**). Trade had become one of the chief causes of rivalry between nations.

Where goods imported to England came from in the later Middlc Agcs.

Assessment tasks

A *Knowledge and understanding*

1 Describe the differe,.t ways in which life in a medieval town was full of danger. Can you think of any ways in which it might have been *less* dangerous than living in a town today?

2 Compare town life and trade in medieval England with that of Roman Britain. Here are some things to consider:

- houses and shops
- the layout of towns
- plays and other public entertainments
- roads and transport
- overseas trade.

3 Source 3 describes one side of London life. Sources 10 and 11 show us another. Here are two more sources about medieval London.

> Everyone shall keep clean the front of his dwelling... pig-sties that are in the streets shall be speedily removed and no pigs are to be found in the streets ... No tavern or ale-house keeper shall keep the door open after curfew has rung ... [at which time] no person shall be so daring as to be found walking through the streets.
> (Regulations for London streets 1297)

> There is no country in the world where there are so many thieves and robbers ... that few venture to go alone ... in the towns at night, and least of all in London ... People are arrested every day by the dozen ... especially in London; yet, for all this, they never cease to rob and murder.
> (Italian visitor, in about 1500)

Write your own account of medieval London life, based on *all five* sources.

B *Interpretations and sources*

4 This artist's impression of life in a medieval town appeared in a school history book published in 1974.

a How far do you think the details in the picture are historically accurate? Give reasons for your answer.

b Compare this picture with other modern illustrations of medieval town life. Can you suggest any reasons why there are often big differences between them?

5 How useful is Source 12 in helping us to understand the relationship between a master and his apprentice? What other things would you have liked to know?

6 Can you think of reasons why the information in Source 24 might not be completely reliable?

9 Troubled times

Black Death and Peasants' Revolt

The year 1348 saw one of the greatest disasters in the whole history of Europe. A terrible plague, which had started in China some years before, swept across the Continent killing millions of people. The plague – known as the Black Death – appeared in the seaports of Italy and southern France at the start of the year and quickly spread inland. It must have been carried by sailors on ships bringing goods from the East. Some people vomited, spat blood and died within a few hours. Others, who seemed to have a different form of the disease, lived a little longer (**Source 1**).

SOURCE 1

One of Italy's greatest writers, Giovanni Boccaccio (1313–75), was living in the city of Florence when it was struck by the plague in the spring of 1348. He described its effects on the people.

In men and women alike it first showed itself by the appearance of certain swellings between the legs or in the armpits, some of which grew as large as a common apple … Black spots or marks like bruises appeared in many cases on the arm or the thigh … Those that recovered [were] few; almost all within three days … sooner or later, died.

SOURCE 2

This picture from a chronicle of the time shows people in Tournai (present-day Belgium) burying their dead during the plague.

The plague comes to Britain

With each new outbreak the plague moved nearer the British Isles. By August it had arrived in the port of Melcombe Regis (now Weymouth) in Dorset. Then it was reported in Bristol. In November it reached London. During the following year (1349) the Black Death spread across England and Wales (**Source 3**). In 1350 it reached Scotland and Ireland.

Dead bodies littered the countryside. It was even worse in the towns, where people lived closer together and were therefore more likely to spread the infection. Town cemeteries were quickly filled. From then on dead bodies were shovelled into deep pits by the cartload (**Source 4**). Some people caught the plague through looking after the sick. But more often sufferers were left to die alone. Husbands and wives parted. There are even reports of parents abandoning their children.

Deaths were not registered in the Middle Ages. So we shall never know exactly how many people were killed by the Black Death. However historians estimate that by the time the plague died down in England, in 1350, about a third of the population had died of it. That amounts to well over 1 million people out of a total of nearly 4 million. The plague returned in 1361–2 and many times after that. But later outbreaks were less severe. Perhaps people developed some resistance to it.

QUESTIONS

1. From the sources on this page, can you work out why the plague was called the Black Death?
2. In Source 2, what impression of the plague is the artist trying to give?
3. Source 3 tells of a shortage of priests. Why do you think priests would have been especially likely to catch the plague?
4. Why might the people of Ashwell (Source 5) have been driven to violence?

SOURCE 3

Henry Knighton, a monk from the abbey of St Mary's in Leicester, lived through the plague. He described its spread as follows.

Then the dreadful plague spread through the coastal regions from Southampton and came to Bristol, and there almost the whole population of the town died, as if overcome by sudden death; for there were few who lived for more than two or three days ... Then this cruel death spread everywhere ... There was such a great shortage of priests that many churches were left abandoned, without divine services.

SOURCE 4

At least half the population of Florence died of the plague in 1348. Boccaccio describes one way of burying the dead.

For each graveyard, as soon as it was full, they dug a huge trench, in which they laid the corpses as they arrived by the hundreds at a time, piling them up as cargo is stored in the hold of a ship, layer upon layer, each covered with a little earth, until the trench would hold no more.

SOURCE 5

This writing was carved on the tower of Ashwell church in Hertfordshire. Part of it reads, in Latin: '1350. Wretched, wild and driven to violence, the remains of the people live to tell the tale.'

The Black Death was probably what modern doctors call the *bubonic plague.* Even today it has not died out completely in parts of Asia. We now know that it was carried by fleas which got on people's bodies from diseased black rats (not the common brown rats familiar in Britain). In medieval times rats were common around the home, living in the roof thatch or even the straw people slept on. The disease could be passed from person to person by the slightest contact. The true cause of the bubonic plague was discovered by scientists only about 100 years ago. In the fourteenth century no one understood what was happening.

Medical ignorance

Medieval people did not know about germs and the way they cause disease. Some guessed that there might be a link between dirt and disease but they did not understand what it could be. So they had little chance of preventing the spread of an infection. And they had even less chance of curing people once they fell ill.

Medicine was not a science in the Middle Ages. It was a mixture of guesswork and superstition. People calling themselves doctors often tried to find cures by studying the movements of the planets. In France, for example, some doctors said the Black Death was caused by the posi-

SOURCE 6

Here we see a woman trying to cure her patient through bleeding. The picture is inside the first letter of a page of writing from a medieval manuscript.

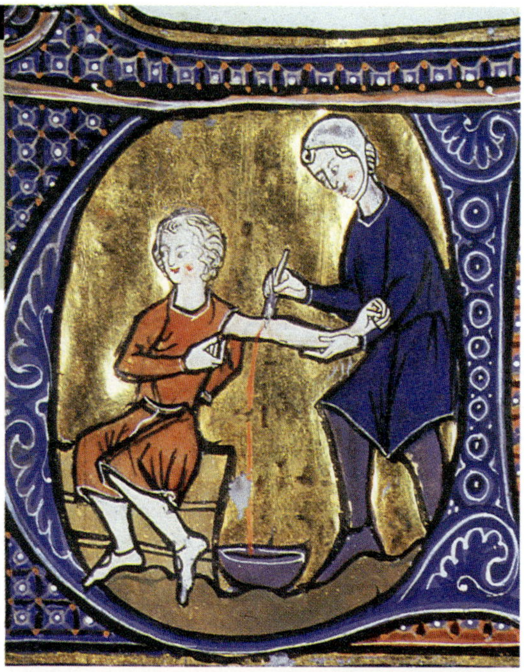

SOURCE 7

Medicines being weighed and mixed. Although most medieval medicines were of no value, some had ingredients that would have helped the patient.

SOURCE 8

These medicines and cures all date from the fourteenth century. The first comes from Wales. It is based on the belief, common at the time, that toothache was caused by worms breeding inside the teeth.

Against toothache Take a candle of mutton-fat, mingled with seed of sea-holly; burn this candle as close as possible to the tooth, holding a basin of cold water beneath it. The worms will fall into the water to escape the heat of the candle.

A good liquid to break the catarrh in a man's head and also a cold in the head Take a red onion and cut it up small, and boil it in a little clary (a mixture of wine and spices) … and add a little honey and … a spoonful of mustard, and boil a long time. Lay the man on his back, and put a little of the mixture in his nose, and let him stand up and sneeze. Do this twice a day for three days and he will be well again.

To cure the Black Death Take a live frog, and lay the belly of it next to the plague sore; if the patient is to escape, the frog will burst in a quarter of an hour; then lay on another; and this you do till more burst, for they draw out the poison. If none of the frogs burst, the person will not escape … Some say a dried toad will do it better.

tion of Jupiter, Saturn and Mars. But doctors also used their common sense, and the better ones learned a lot from experience. When they saw how quickly the plague spread, some tried to keep sick and healthy people apart.

A favourite remedy for many ills was to make the patient bleed. A vein was opened and the 'bad blood' drawn off into a cup (**Source 6**). This might have been useful in some cases, but generally it just made the patient weaker. If blood-letting failed, doctors often turned to remedies which nowadays seem absurd. The sick were given medicines containing anything from herbs and roots to the insides of dead animals. Medieval people often seem to have believed that the nastier the medicine the greater the chance of it doing some good (**Source 8**).

Consequences of the Black Death

Survivors of the plague lived in a changed world. So many people had died that in some villages there was scarcely anyone left to plough the land, sow crops or milk the cows. Such villages were often abandoned. Their buildings fell into ruin and grass grew over the fields. In photographs like the one on page 37 we can still see traces of villages deserted at this time.

For many years, some lords of the manor had been freeing villeins from their feudal services (see page 100). Free men paid the lord rent for their cottage and strips instead of having to work part of the week on his land. The lord then used the money to hire labourers to work for him. Labourers living on wages were more reliable than villeins who often tried to dodge the work they owed the lord.

After the plague, however, labourers were in short supply. They soon realised their increased value and demanded higher wages. Lords were forced to pay up or see their crops rot in the fields. Parliament, which contained many lords but no peasants, tried to put a stop to such demands. It ordered that wages were to remain as they had been before the plague. This made working people angry and did not stop them demanding higher pay (**Source 9**).

Meanwhile, those who were still villeins were keener than ever to buy their freedom and try to better themselves. But many lords refused to release them. While workers were scarce and wages rising,

SOURCE 9

The chronicler Henry Knighton here describes what happened when the King's council tried to keep down wages.

Labourers were so sure of themselves and obstinate that they did not listen to the King's command. If anyone wanted to employ them he would have to pay them what they wanted ... When the King was told that abbots, priors, knights ... and others, great and small, throughout the countryside ... were not obeying his order, and had given higher wages to their workers, he imposed heavy fines on them ... Then the King had many labourers arrested, and sent them to prison.

SOURCE 10

John Ball (see page 94). This is part of a book illustration dating from about 1460 – nearly eighty years after his death.

lords often held on to what they had got. They strictly enforced labour services and brought slackers before the manor court to be punished (see **Source 7** on page 41). Such treatment made villeins bitter and restless.

Many villeins who were refused their freedom ran away. Since the plague it was easy to find work in a town or on another manor. Peasants in some areas were stirred up against their lords by priests. One such priest, John Ball, became well known in the counties around London. He preached that it was wrong for the rich to live off the work of the common people because at the beginning of the world everyone was equal (**Source 11**). John Ball spread discontent for twenty years before the Church authorities finally put him in prison.

SOURCE 11

This comes from the *Chronicle* of Jean Froissart, a Frenchman who often travelled to England in these years.

A mad priest in the county of Kent, John Ball by name, [would] collect a crowd ... and address them more or less as follows: 'My friends, the state of England cannot be right until ... there is no difference between nobleman and serf ... They are dressed in velvet and furs, while we wear only poor clothing ... They have fine houses and manors, and we have to brave the wind and rain as we toil in the fields ... Let us go to the King. He is young, and we will show him our miserable slavery; we will tell him it must be changed, or else we will provide the remedy ourselves.

SOURCE 12

This wooden likeness of King Edward III at the time of his death is in Westminster Abbey. Half French by birth, Edward claimed he had a right to the French Crown and declared war on the King of France in 1337. This was the start of a long series of raids and English invasions, with periods of peace in between, which lasted until 1453. Historians call it 'The Hundred Years War', although the actual fighting amounted to much less than 100 years.

The Revolt of 1381

King Edward III (1327–77) loved the excitement of war and spent much of his reign fighting the king of France. Edward was successful at first, but in his later years he suffered defeats and lost many of his French lands. Heavy taxes were raised to pay for these wars. This made the people of England even more discontented.

On Edward's death, the Crown passed to his ten-year old son, Richard II. This meant that for a few years the kingdom would have to be ruled by a council of nobles. Most of them were very unpopular. To carry on the French war, it was ordered in November 1380 that everyone over fifteen must pay a *poll tax*. Poll means head; in other words every head, or person, had to pay. There had been a poll tax of fourpence in 1377 and 1379. But now

QUESTIONS

1 In the medicine for catarrh (Source 8) can you find any ingredients we might still use today?

2 Do you think the punishments mentioned in Source 9 were fair? Give reasons for your answer.

3 John Ball is often remembered for these words:

When Adam delved (dug the ground)
and Eve span,
Who was then a gentleman?

Can you explain what he meant?

4 Why do you think priests in particular often spoke out against rich lords?

the tax averaged twelve pence. A husband and wife alone would have to find at least a week's wages between them.

When royal officials came to collect the tax, many people were hiding. The amount gathered was much less than expected. So new collectors were recruited in the spring of 1381 and sent to root out the tax dodgers. In parts of Essex and Kent crowds drove them away and the 'Peasants' Revolt' had begun. Actually it was much more than a revolt of peasants. Many town tradesmen joined in, along with discontented priests, friars and outlaws.

On both sides of the river Thames men armed themselves. Some had longbows; others made do with scythes, sickles or knives. The rebels chose as their leader a man named Wat Tyler who had been a soldier in France. Their plan was to march to London and put their demands to King Richard, now aged fourteen. They thought of him as the true leader of the common people and blamed their troubles on landlords, tax-gatherers and the King's hated advisers. There were probably at least 50,000 rebels altogether. On the way to London they freed prisoners from jails, among them John Ball who had been held at Maidstone.

On 13 June the rebels entered London without striking a blow. Gates on both sides of the city were opened by supporters inside. Tyler had given orders against theft and disorderly behaviour, but not all his men followed them (**Source 14**). The King and his advisers, meanwhile, had gone to the Tower of London for safety. They now realised that their only hope was for the King to meet the rebels.

Early next day Richard, with a bodyguard of soldiers, rode to meet Wat Tyler in the fields of Mile End outside the city. Tyler put forward the rebels' demands, which included the freeing of all villeins. Richard had little choice but to agree. Without delay, thirty clerks began writing charters of freedom for peasants to take back to their lords.

SOURCE 13

King Richard II holding the orb and sceptre – symbols of the royal power. This was probably painted from life in about 1390. It is the earliest known painting of an English monarch. Richard had an unhappy reign. He made many enemies among the nobles and in the end lost the throne to his cousin Henry (1399) and was murdered.

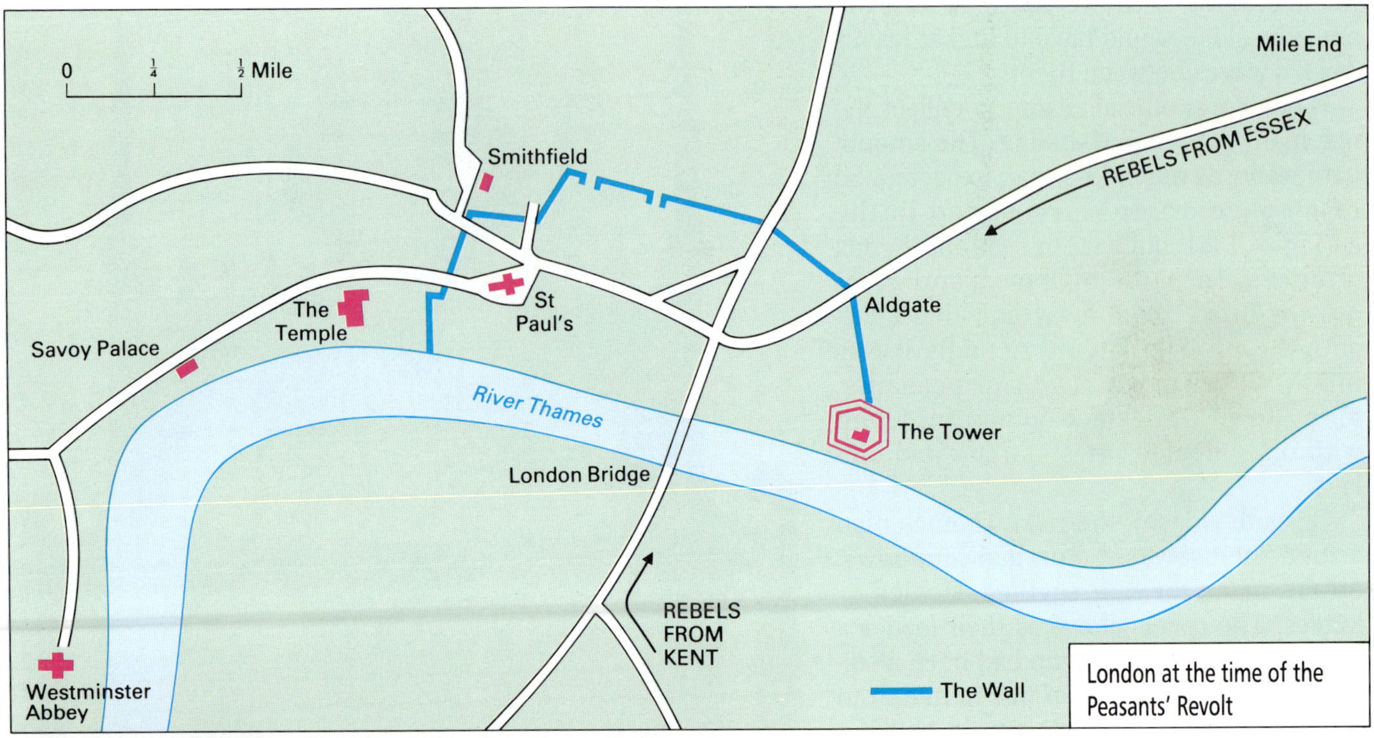

London at the time of the Peasants' Revolt

SOURCE 14

This account comes from the *Anonimal* (anonymous, or nameless) *Chronicle* of the abbey of St Mary's, York. Parts of it, including this passage, were probably written by an eyewitness.

The rebels made their way through the middle of London, and did no harm or damage until … the men of Kent broke open the prison in Fleet Street and turned out all the prisoners … [At] the house of the Bishop of Chester … they rolled barrels of wine out of his cellar, and drunk their fill … At last they came to the Savoy (home of the King's uncle, John of Gaunt) … And they burnt the hall and the chambers, and all the buildings inside the gates of the palace … The rebels from Kent were blamed for this arson, but some said the Londoners were really guilty, because of their hatred of the Duke.

QUESTIONS

1. Why do you think the peasants trusted King Richard to treat them fairly?
2. Can you think of reasons why the rebels freed prisoners from jails?
3. Does Source 14 help to explain why the rebels were eventually outsmarted?
4. Is there any clue in Source 14 as to why the rebels found it so easy to enter London?

Many peasants went home once they had written proof of the King's promises. But the leaders stayed in London, still backed by powerful forces. Another meeting with Richard was arranged for 15 June at Smithfield. Here Tyler made further demands. He wanted lords' estates reduced in size and Church lands divided among the people. Again, Richard agreed. Tyler got on his pony to ride back across the field. At that moment one of the King's followers shouted insults at the rebel leader. A scuffle broke out and another of the royal party ran Tyler through with his sword.

The King's attendants may have planned to kill Tyler, though we shall never know for sure. When the rebel army realised what had happened, they loaded their longbows. But before they could shoot at the King's followers, Richard rode towards the peasant ranks and called out to them to stop. The rebels still trusted Richard. They lowered their weapons and followed him into fields nearby. There he repeated his promises and talked them into going home. It was a great triumph for the boy king.

SOURCE 15

While Wat Tyler and King Richard were meeting at Mile End, a band of rebels entered the Tower of London. They dragged out the Archbishop of Canterbury and ministers who were blamed for the poll tax. This illustration dating from about 1460 shows the rebels' victims being executed on Tower Hill. As the Archbishop kneels (left) his bishop's hat, or *mitre*, falls to the ground. It was later nailed to his skull when his head was stuck on London Bridge.

SOURCE 16

The end of the Peasants' Revolt. This comes from the same book as Sources 10 and 15. The artist has combined two incidents in one. On the left Wat Tyler is attacked while King Richard watches; on the right the King rides towards the rebel ranks. The artist has made the peasants look like a proper army, but in real life very few of them would have had any sort of armour.

Worthless promises

Once the rebels were safely out of London, royal forces tracked down the ringleaders. Soldiers first marched into Essex. Everywhere the charters granted to villeins proved worthless (**Source 17**). At Chelmsford, a group of rebel leaders was sentenced and hanged. The same happened at Colchester, where there was such a shortage of gallows that nineteen men were reported hanging from one beam. In Kent, too, many rebel leaders were executed.

The main centres of the Peasants' Revolt in south-eastern England.

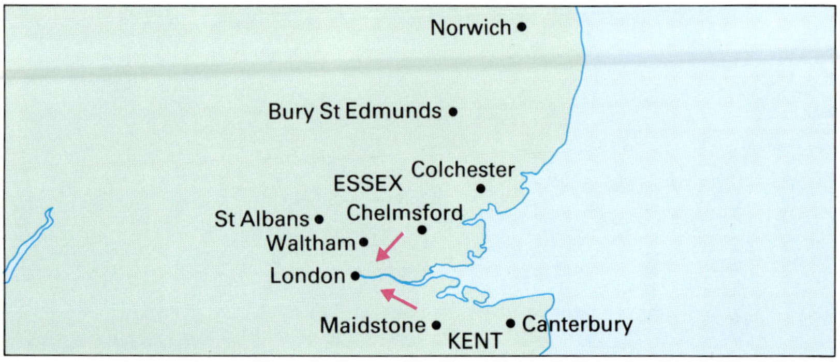

SOURCE 17

At Waltham, in Essex, the King told peasants that promises obtained by force counted for nothing. According to the chronicler of St Albans abbey, Thomas Walsingham, Richard spoke harshly.

Oh you wretched men ... you who seek to be equal with lords are not worthy to live! ... Villeins you were, and villeins you shall remain ... For as long as we live, and by God's grace, rule over the realm, we shall strive ... to keep you down so that the hardships you suffer will be an example to those who come after. Now and in the future, people of your kind will always ... fear to copy the things you have done.

SOURCE 18

The *Anonimal Chronicle* tells us that at the very end the young King showed the rebels some mercy.

The King sent out his messengers ... to capture the wrongdoers and put them to death. And many were taken and hanged in London ... and in other cities and boroughs of the south country. At last, as it pleased God, the King, seeing that too many of his subjects would be undone, and too much blood spilt, took pity in his heart, and granted them all pardon, on condition that they should never rise again ... And so finished this wicked war.

There was much more to the Peasants' Revolt than the events in Essex, Kent and London. The rising spread right across south-eastern England and there were disturbances as far north as York and as far west as Devon. The town of St Albans, in Hertfordshire, was on the estates of an abbot who had long refused to free his villeins. On 15 June, the day of Wat Tyler's death, the citizens rioted. They drained the abbot's fishponds, freed prisoners from his jail and divided his estates among themselves.

The abbot of St Albans was forced to sign a charter freeing all his villeins. But their rejoicing was short-lived. A few weeks later the King arrived with an army. Fifteen rebels were tried and hanged. With them died John Ball. He had been captured in Coventry and taken to St Albans for trial. He openly admitted his guilt and refused to beg the King for pardon.

Another town on the estates of an abbey was Bury St Edmunds, in Suffolk. Here rebels led by a priest, John Wraw, beheaded the prior of the abbey and one of the King's Chief Justices, Sir John Cavendish. But ten days later Wraw was defeated by royal troops, taken to London and hanged. In the neighbouring county of Norfolk, rebels led by a dyer, Geoffrey Litster, captured Norwich. They lived in the castle and made knights serve them at table. However the Bishop of Norwich, Henry Despenser, had other ideas. He put on his armour and quickly gathered an army of local landowners. He then defeated Litster's forces and saw their leader put to death.

By the end of August the revolt had been completely crushed (**Source 18**). It seemed that the rebels had failed and that many had died for nothing. But a revolt as big as that of 1381 was bound to leave its mark. There were no more poll taxes in medieval England and Parliament soon gave up all attempts to keep down wages. Within fifty years, nearly all villeins had been given their freedom.

Assessment tasks

A *Knowledge and understanding*

1 a Is there anything the people of the British Isles could have done to avoid the Black Death? Why do you think such action was not taken?

b What were the consequences of the Black Death for England, (i) in the short term, and (ii) in the long term?

2 Look back over this chapter and list all the causes of the Peasants' Revolt. Then divide them into two kinds:

a *political* causes (decisions by those in power – the King and nobles);

b *social* causes (resulting from the peasants' daily lives).

3 Here are four possible reasons why the Peasants' Revolt failed. You may wish to add others.

- The rebels were loyal to King Richard.
- They did not know what to do once they were in control.
- They trusted the King and nobles to keep their promises.
- Wat Tyler was killed.

Which do you think is the most important reason, and why?

B *Interpretations and sources*

4 Here are two different views of the lives of peasants at the time of the Revolt. In the first, written about 1375, John Gower, a poet and wealthy landowner, foretold the troubles that lay ahead in England. The second comes from a book written six centuries later, in 1987, by Brian Bird, a Church of England priest.

> The world goes fast from bad to worse, when shepherd and cowherd demand more for their work than the master-bailiff used to get in days gone by ... Labourers of old were not used to eating wheat bread; theirs was made of beans or rougher corn, and their drink was of water alone ... I see the poor folk more haughty (proud) than their lords ... [They] show no mercy when they get the upper hand.

> It must be remembered that the working people at this time were living in a state of near-slavery. They possessed few rights, and were treated by lords and nobility not much better than animals, to be disposed of like chattels (goods) ... They wanted freedom from crippling taxes ... the right to be taken on as free tenants of their land at a fair rent ... and to receive payments for work done for their lords.

Why do you think these two writers see things so differently?

5 a In Sources 9, 11 and 18, what clues are there that these were written from the lords' point of view?

b There is no known account of the rebels' view of the Peasants' Revolt. Can you suggest any reasons for this?

6 Look again at the fifteenth-century pictures of scenes from the Peasants' Revolt (Sources 15 and 16). How useful are they in helping us to understand what happened?

10 The English realm

Changes in village life, language and religion

We saw in the last chapter that lords of the manor started freeing villeins from labour services well before the Black Death. Free men paid rent for their cottage and strips in the fields instead of having to work on the lord's land. By 1500, this change had occurred almost everywhere in England (**Source 1**). However it did not mean the end of 'open field' farming. In many villages free men still worked together to farm their scattered strips. There had been little change in farming methods and crops since the Norman Conquest.

SOURCE 1

This document, which records the freeing of a villein, was issued by the abbot of the monastery of Peterborough in 1449.

Let it be known to all that we have … caused to be free William Clopton of Greatford … with all his children, born and to be born, with his goods and belongings, granting full freedom to them for ever, so that neither we nor our servants … shall in future be able to demand or claim any right over William and his children.

The break-up of the manor

The Black Death of 1348–9 probably reduced the population of England and Wales from just under 4 million to about $2^1/_2$ million. (This compares with 50 million today). The plague returned to England many times. Later outbreaks had much less effect, but they were enough to keep the population down. It was still no more than 3 million in 1500.

The fall in the population meant that there was spare farming land on most manors. Hard-working peasants who had saved a little money saw their chance to buy or rent extra strips. These better-off villagers, with more land than ordinary peasants, were known as *yeoman* farmers. As their land-holdings grew in size they hired labourers to work for them.

Some yeomen exchanged strips in the open fields with their neighbours so as to get their land together in one piece. It could then be enclosed with hedges and ditches and made into a single farm.

SOURCE 2

The ending of labour services on the manor meant that coins like these became more important in village life. Free men had to sell some of their produce to pay their rent, and lords paid wages to their labourers.

SOURCE 3

Sheep in a pen. This is another illustration from the Luttrell Psalter (see Source 6 on page 40).

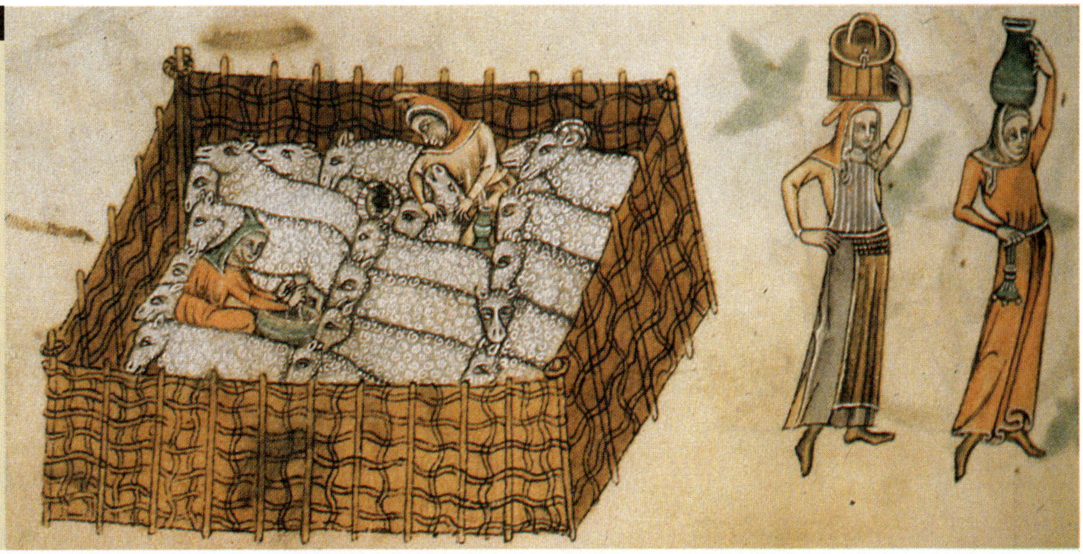

SOURCE 4

At Stretton Baskerville in Warwickshire, the turning of ploughland into pasture destroyed the village in 1493. This account comes from a survey of enclosures made 25 years later.

Henry Smith … enclosed the cottages, gardens and fields with ditches and banks and he wilfully caused the same cottages and their plots to be demolished and laid waste and he converted them … into pasture for brute animals … As a result 12 ploughs that were employed in farming those lands are removed and 80 persons … forced to depart tearfully against their will. Since then they have remained idle and thus they lead a miserable life.

QUESTIONS

1. In Source 1, the villein's present and future children are mentioned but not his wife. Can you explain why?
2. What would have been the advantages, from a lord's point of view, of turning plough-land over to pasture?
3. In Source 3, what products from sheep are the women on the right carrying? There is a clue on the left of the picture.
4. In Source 4, which side is the writer on: Henry Smith's or the villagers'? Give reasons for your answer.

Lords, too, were often keen to enclose their lands. In some areas it paid them to turn plough-land over to pasture, enclose it and keep sheep and cattle. Sheep-farming was especially profitable because of the great demand for wool.

The enclosure of land for sheep-farming meant far fewer workers were needed. Ploughing, sowing and reaping crops was work for many hands, but two or three shepherds could look after a large area of pasture. This suited lords very well, but it led to the ruin of many village communities. Often peasants' cottages were pulled down to clear the land, leaving families homeless and without work (**Source 4**). Many took to begging to stay alive.

'Frensche into Englische'

There were three different languages in medieval England. Latin was written and spoken by educated people, nearly all of them churchmen. Most books were in Latin and it was the basis of schooling. French was the language of the kings and lords who ruled England after the Norman Conquest. Only peasants and tradesmen – the descendants of the conquered Anglo-Saxons – kept English alive.

However the nobles and lesser lords began to change from French to English during the fourteenth century. By then the 'Norman French' used in England had become very different from the French

SOURCE 5

Henry IV (1399–1413). He was the first king of England since 1066 whose native language was English.

SOURCE 6

In 1349 a schoolmaster named John Cornwall began to get his pupils to translate their Latin books into English instead of French. This account, in the original spelling, was written by a Cornish priest, John of Trevisa, in 1385.

John Cornwaile, a maister of grammar, chaunged [from] Frensche into Englische … so that now … in alle the gramere scoles of Engelond, children leveth Frensche … and lerneth an Englische … Here avauntage is that they lerneth ther gramer in lasse tyme than children were i-woned to doo; disavauntage is that now children of gramer scole conneth (know) na more Frensche than thir left heele (left heel).

spoken in France. French people thought it odd and old-fashioned and had begun to laugh at it! A further reason for the decline of the French language in England was anti-French feeling caused by war between the two kingdoms.

When Edward III began the 'Hundred Years War' against the King of France in 1337, he did not think of it as a contest between 'English' and 'foreigners'. Edward was half French himself and had close ties with France. But as the fighting went on attitudes changed. By the end of the war, in 1453, all the French lands belonging to the English Crown had been lost, apart from the town of Calais. This gave English people a stronger sense of belonging to a separate nation, with its own customs and language.

English became the language of the law-courts in 1362. Next year Parliament was opened in English for the first time. By then, English was already entering the school-room (**Source 6**). French did not disappear completely. Many French words – and Latin ones too – blended with English. The change to English was not easy because there were many different versions, or *dialects*, of the language. Traces of these live on in England today, but in medieval times people from different parts of the country often could not understand each other.

The dialect spoken in London gradually came to be understood all over the kingdom. An important reason for this was its use by the poet Geoffrey Chaucer (1340–1400). Chaucer became famous throughout the land for his *Canterbury Tales* – a collection of stories in verse told by a party of pilgrims travelling to Thomas Becket's shrine (see page 34). Educated people not only read Chaucer but also the works of poets who copied his style. In this way they learned the London dialect and tried to use it themselves in letters and other writings (**Source 8**).

English in print

The popularity of Chaucer's works helped to fix a single form of English. A further step towards a common language came with the invention of the printing press. Johannes Gutenberg, a citizen of Mainz in Germany, produced Europe's first printed book in about 1450. Previously it had only been possible to print pictures carved on wooden blocks, but Gutenberg used movable type to set up pages of writing. The Chinese craft of making paper from linen rag had recently been learned in Europe. Paper cost a lot less to make than parchment. The two inventions of printing and paper made books much cheaper.

A wealthy English merchant, William Caxton, set up England's first printing press in London in 1476. During the previous thirty years he had been living in Bruges (in present-day Belgium). His hobby was to collect and translate books. When he heard about the invention of printing in Germany, he went there to learn about it. Caxton built a press when he got back to Bruges, and it was there that he printed the first books in English, in 1475.

In his London workshop, close to Westminster Abbey, Caxton printed more than ninety different books. Most were in

SOURCE 7

Geoffrey Chaucer, from an illustrated copy of his *Canterbury Tales.* He was the son of a London merchant and, for a time, worked in the service of King Edward III. Unlike most other poets of his time, Chaucer wrote only in English.

SOURCE 8

Here, in the original spelling, is part of a love letter dating from 1477. It was written for St Valentine's Day by Margery Brews, a Norfolk landowner's daughter, to her sweetheart, John Paston. They were married later the same year.

Ryght reverent and wurschypfull, and my ryght wele-beloved Voluntyne (Valentine), I recomande me unto yowe, ffull hertely desyring to here of yowr welefare, wheche I beseche Almyghty God long for to preserve un to Hys plesur, and yowr herts desyre. And yf it please yowe to here of my welefar, I am not in good heele (health) of body, nor of herte, nor schall be tyll I her ffrom yowe.

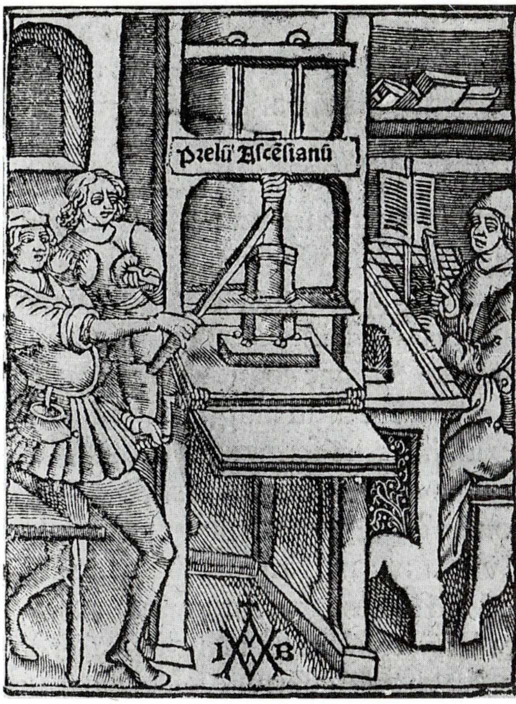

SOURCE 9

This is the oldest known picture of a printing press. It comes from a book printed in Paris in 1507. Can you work out what the person on the right is doing?

SOURCE 10

The story of the Fox and the Grapes from an edition of Aesop's *Fables* printed by John Caxton. This is one of the earliest printed book illustrations.

Liber quartus Folio lxvij

¶ The fyrst fable maketh mencyon of the foxe and of the raysyns

He is not wyse/ that desyreth to haue a thynge whiche he may not haue/ As recyteth this fable Of a foxe/ whiche loked and behelde the raysyns that grewe vpon an hyghe vyne/ the whiche raysyns he moche desyred for to ete them ¶ And whanne he sawe that none he myght gete/ he torned his sorowe in to Ioye/ and sayd these raysyns ben sowre/ and yf I had some I wold not ete them/ And therfore this fable sheweth that he is wyse / whiche fayneth not to desyre that thynge the whiche he may not haue/

¶ The second fable is of the auncyent wesel and of the rat/

Wytte is better than force or strengthe / As reherceth to vs this fable of an old wesel / the whiche myghte no more take no rats/ wherfor she was ofte sore hongry

i iij

SOURCE 11

This comes from an introduction Caxton wrote for one of his printed books which he translated himself from French into English. It is in the original spelling.

That comyn englysshe that is spoken in one shyre (county) varyeth from another. In so moche that in my dayes happened that certayn marchauntes (merchants) were in a shippe in Tamyse (river Thames) ... and wente to lande for to refreshe them; And one of theym ... cam in-to an hows and axed for mete (food); and specyally he axyed after eggys; and the goode wyf answerde that she coude speke no frenshe. And the marchaunt was angry, for he coude speke no frenshe . . . And theene at laste another sayd that he wolde haue 'eyren', then the good wyf sayd that she vnderstod hym wel. Loo, what sholde a man in thyse dayes now wryte, 'egges' or 'eyren'?

English, some of them translated by Caxton himself. Other presses were soon set up, at Oxford in 1478 and St Albans in 1480. Early books took much longer to print than modern ones. Each page of type had to be assembled and inked by hand. Sales of such books were very small by present-day standards. Most people in Caxton's day could neither read books nor afford to buy them.

There were no dictionaries in those

SOURCE 12, 13 and 14

In *The Canterbury Tales*, the poor priest practised what he preached. But the monk and friar seemed more interested in the pleasures of life than the service of God.

12 A good man was ther of religioun,
And was a povre persoun (poor parson) of a toun,
But riche he was of hooly thoght and werk.
He was also a lerned man, a clerk ...
To drawen folk to hevene by fairnesse,
By good ensample (example), this was his bisynesse ...
But Cristes loore (teaching) and his apostles twelve
He taughte, but first he folwed it hymselve.

13 A monk ther was ... to been an abbot able.
Ful many a deyntee (valuable) hors hadde he in stable ...
Grehoundes he hadde as swift as fowel in flight;
Of prikyng (tracking) and of huntyng for the hare
Was al his lust (desire), for no cost wolde he spare.

14 A frere (friar) ther was ... lyk a maister (lord) or a pope.
Of double worstede (fine cloth) was his semycope (cloak) ...
He knew the tavernes wel in every toun
And everich hostiler (every innkeeper) and tappestere (barmaid) ....
He was the beste beggere in his hous.

days, so Caxton had to decide for himself what the form and spelling of English should be. Like Chaucer, he used the dialect he knew – that of the London area. Even so, he realised that there were parts of the country where it would not be properly understood (**Source 11**). Caxton did much to bring about a 'standard English', but it did not become the language of all the people until long after his death.

John Wyclif and the Lollards

The pilgrims in Chaucer's *Canterbury Tales* would have been based on people he had met. Several belong to the Church, including a priest, friar, monk and the prioress of a nunnery. Chaucer's description of these characters tells us a lot about the Church in his lifetime. He admired the humble parish priest, but made fun of the other religious characters because they did not live as strictly as they were supposed to (**Sources 12–14**).

In Chaucer's day, monks and friars still praised God and did good works. But they often ignored the rules of St Benedict and St Francis (see Chapter 3). Friars lived in comfortable homes and begged for money – which St Francis had strictly forbidden. Monks frequently found excuses to miss church services and go outside their monasteries.

A leading teacher at Oxford University, John Wyclif (1320–84), openly criticised the Church. He said it was wrong for God's servants to have so many lands and possessions. (At that time the estates of Church lords covered a fifth of the kingdom). Wyclif said that Christians should ignore the Pope, the bishops and all other churchmen who went against Christ's example and lived in luxury (**Source 15**). He also refused to believe the Church's teaching that during the communion service the bread and wine on the altar changed into the real flesh and blood of Christ.

SOURCE 15

In this extract from Wyclif's writings, the original English spelling has been modernised.

Christ was a most poor man from his birth to his death, and shunned (avoided) worldly riches ... Anti-Christ (the Pope) by contrast ... covets (desires) to be worldly rich ... Christ was the most meek (humble) of men ... but men say that the pope is the most proud man on earth, and makes lords kiss his feet, whereas Christ washed His Apostles' feet ... And if you should say that Christ's Church must have a Head here on earth, true it is, for ... Christ not the pope is Head of the Church.

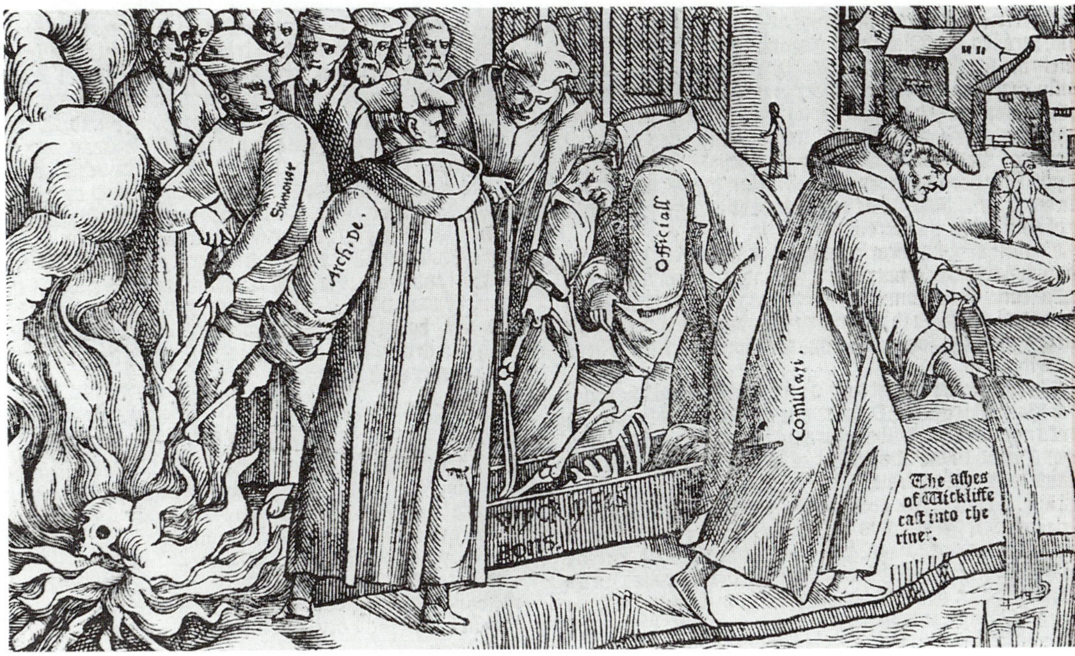

SOURCE 16

Wyclif died peacefully, at Lutterworth in Leicestershire. But when his views became more widely known he was condemned by the Church. More than 40 years after his death, his body was dug up, burnt to ashes and thrown in a river – as this picture shows.

Wyclif and some of his Oxford friends translated the Bible from Latin into English. They wanted more people to be able to read it for themselves and not have to depend on what the Church saw fit to tell them. Church leaders were strongly against the Bible being translated. They said that only churchmen could understand its true meaning and it was their task to explain it to people.

The first English Bible was finished in 1382. Wyclif died two years later, but his attack on the Church was not forgotten. A number of 'Poor Preachers' began spreading his ideas. They spoke to gatherings of people in towns and villages and read to them from the English Bible. Their enemies in the Church called them Lollards (babblers or mumblers). Many Lollards were arrested and put in prison. Some who refused to accept the teachings of the Church were burnt to death (**Source 17**).

SOURCE 17

A Lollard called John Badby was one of many who followed Wyclif in denying that the bread and wine in the communion service was the real body of Christ. The chronicler Thomas Walsingham tells us what happened to him, in 1410. The 'lord prince' referred to was the future King Henry V.

He was condemned, and enclosed in a barrel in Smithfield ... and groaned miserably amidst the burning. The lord prince was moved by his pitiful cries, and ordered ... the man to be removed from the flames. He comforted the half-dead man and promised him even now life and pardon, and a grant of threepence a day from the royal treasury, if he would repent; but the unhappy man refused the offer ... Wherefore the lord prince ordered him to be enclosed once more in the barrel ... and so the foolish man was burnt to ashes.

SOURCE 18

Lollards being executed in Coventry. At first, Lollards were thought to be lunatics and not many people took them seriously. But in 1401 Parliament imposed severe penalties, including death, on those who challenged the teachings of the Church.

QUESTIONS

1. What is Chaucer saying about the friar (Source 14) when he describes him as the best beggar in his house?
2. What are Wyclif's reasons for calling the Pope 'Anti-Christ' (Source 15)?
3. In Source 17, what do you think is the writer's view of the events he is describing? Give reasons for your answer.
4. What does Source 17 tell you about the attitudes of the Lollards?

Lollards were forced to meet in secret. But they still had many supporters, especially among tradespeople in the larger towns. Few of these had any schooling, so they often had to find someone to read to them from Lollard books or the English Bible. The Lollards allowed women as well as men to preach. This was forbidden by the Church and women who were found out often paid for their beliefs with their lives.

Critics of the Church would not be silenced – either in England or on the Continent. Growing numbers of Christians believed that if churchmen did not live holy lives themselves they had no right to preach to others. In the sixteenth century several rulers, including Henry VIII of England, broke away from the Church of Rome and set up reformed churches in their own countries.

A time of change

History is a story of continual change. However the speed of change is not always the same. Sometimes it quickens. One such time in England was the century between about 1450 and 1550. These years saw the end of feudal lordship and of a single Christian Church under the Pope; the foundations of medieval life crumbled away. At the same time other vital changes occurred. The use of gunpowder began to change the nature of warfare, and the

SOURCE 19

Henry V (1413–22). Like his father, Henry IV, he strongly supported the bishops in their attack upon the Lollards. However he is better remembered for a great victory over the French at the battle of Agincourt (1415).

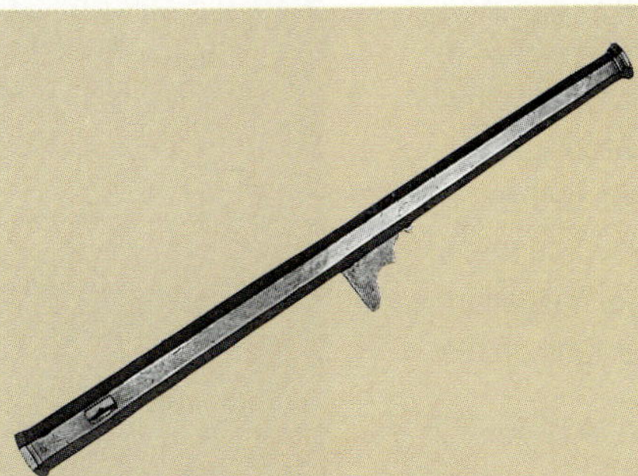

SOURCE 20

A fifteenth-century hand gun. The first use of gunpowder in Europe was with cannon, in the previous century, but the earliest cannon often burst and were a greater threat to the gunners than the enemy.

printing press speeded up the spread of knowledge and ideas.

Meanwhile on the high seas it was an age of exploration and discovery. A turning point came in 1492 when an Italian sea-captain, Cristoforo Columbus, crossed the Atlantic Ocean to the West Indies. Columbus's discovery opened up a 'New World' to the people of Europe. The British Isles had much to gain from it. Previously they had been a long way from the world's main trading routes. But in future they would be at the heart of things, as sea trade with the Americas grew.

It is for reasons like these that historians usually date the end of the Middle Ages – and the start of modern history – somewhere between 1450 and 1550. This book does not go beyond 1500. But of course that does not mean the 'medieval' way of life it describes ended in a particular year (**Source 21**).

SOURCE 22

On the Thursday before Easter every year, the monarch visits one of the great churches to give 'Maundy' money to pensioners. Originally food and clothing were given to the poor and the monarch washed their feet, just as Christ washed his disciples' feet at the Last Supper. The first known Maundy ceremony was performed by King John in 1210 – as this extract from his accounts shows.

On the day of the Lord's Supper in Knaresborough (Yorkshire) in Maundy (gifts) from the King to 13 poor people, 13 pence [each] ... For the robes of these poor people ... and for their robes to be sewn: 2 shillings, 2 pence. For 13 belts, 13 knives, 13 pairs of drawers (pants) ... and for 13 pairs of shoes totalling 14 shillings 1½ pence paid by the abbot of Bindon.

SOURCE 21

King Henry VII (1485–1509). Historians sometimes date the end of the Middle Ages in England from the year Henry became king. This is because he ended the so-called Wars of the Roses by defeating and killing King Richard III (1483–85) at the battle of Bosworth. For 30 years previously two rival groups of nobles had fought for the Crown. One had as its badge the white rose of the Duke of York and the other later took up the red rose.

The medieval world around us

Five hundred years after Caxton and Columbus, there is still much to remind us of the Middle Ages. In Britain and Europe, many people still worship in medieval churches and cathedrals, or spend their leisure time visiting the remains of castles and abbeys. Inside the great churches, the work of medieval craftsmen lives on in fine carvings of wood, stone and brass.

Some customs from the Middle Ages have lasted as long as its stone buildings. For instance, May Day celebrations, morris dancing, Pancake Day and the giving of Maundy money by the monarch (**Source 22**) all began in those far-off times. Moreover British law and government still have roots deep in the Middle Ages. Judges wearing medieval robes travel round the counties as Henry II's justices did over 800 years ago. In the courts, twelve ordinary people still make up the jury.

Kings and queens have lost the power they once had. But they are still crowned at Westminster, like William the Conqueror. Power has now shifted to the Houses of Parliament. In the Commons, MPs grant taxes just as knights and burgesses did long ago. In the Lords, the Chancellor sits on the Woolsack, a reminder of the source of England's wealth in medieval times. Even local councils, mayors and aldermen date from the Middle Ages.

In many countries, such traditions have been swept away by military invasion or revolution. This has not happened to the British people. Their strong links with the past give them an added reason to know about their history.

SOURCE 23

Morris dancing in the centre of Oxford – part of the city's May Morning celebrations which date back to medieval times.

SOURCE 24

The Lord Mayor's Show. Every year, on the second Saturday of November, the newly-elected Lord Mayor of London travels in a procession through the City before swearing loyalty to the monarch. The oath of loyalty goes back to 1215, when King John granted a charter to London giving its people the right to elect a mayor.

Assessment tasks

A *Knowledge and understanding*

1 Make a timeline of important dates in the development of the English language. Include not just events in particular years but also things that happened over longer periods of time.

2 a Using the information in this chapter, make a list of important changes or happenings in the fifteenth century that affected the lives of English people.

b Did all these changes make life better or might some have made it worse? Give reasons for your answer.

3 Find out what remains of the Middle Ages in your area. The illustrations in this book may give you some clues. Things to consider include buildings (such as churches and castles) and their contents, objects preserved in museums, and customs that are kept going from year to year.

B *Interpretations and sources*

4 Look again at Sources 23 and 24 – and also Source 13 on page 83.

a What picture of medieval life do you think people get from events of this kind?

b How far is it a true picture?

c In what other ways do people in their everyday lives form views or impressions of the medieval world?

5 a Write out Source 8 in modern English spelling.

b What does it tell you about relationships between men and women at the time?

6 Re-read Source 11 carefully.

a Why do you think Caxton chose to tell this story in a book he had translated into English?

b When the woman heard a word she did not understand, why did she think it must be French?

c How would the work of Caxton and other printers help to reduce this kind of misunderstanding in future?

Index

Topics in the National Curriculum Orders are in bold type.
Page numbers in *italics* refer to illustrations.

KELMSCOTT MANOR: THE PLACE TODAY

'A house that I love with a reasonable love I think'

William Morris

Kelmscott Manor is a rambling, limestone-built farmhouse that was the country home of writer and designer William Morris from 1871 until his death in 1896. It was also home to his wife Jane ('Janey') and their children Jenny and May, and his friend, poet, and artist Dante Gabriel Rossetti, shared it with them from 1871 until 1874.

William Morris's life and work as creator, poet, designer, conservationist, and socialist campaigner have made Kelmscott Manor internationally famous, and for Morris it was a source of emotional and artistic inspiration. He thought of it as 'a heaven on earth', and felt renewed by its beauty and quiet, once writing to a friend: 'the ancient house had me in its arms again'. He claimed to love 'the Earth through that small space of it'.

Today, the house is owned and protected by the Society of Antiquaries of London as a place for visitors to appreciate its architecture, setting and rich history, as well as a base for research and conservation. It is open to the public, which allows visitors to explore the threads of imaginative creativity and art that unfold from the story of Morris, his family and his circle, and to look into the deeper history of an English farmstead and the rural way of life.

Recent research has helped further our understanding of the house and its contents, by analysing the details of the building itself, early photographs and watercolour sketches, as well as key documentary sources. These include inventories of the house made in 1611 at the death of Thomas Turner, in 1833 at the death of Charles Turner, and in 1870, before Morris took on the lease after the death of James Turner, as well as the detailed memorandum of contents drawn up by May Morris in 1926. Other key sources are an 1895 sketch plan by Morris's friend, the architect Philip Webb, and a detailed survey made in 1964 before a major restoration.

The village settlement around the house remains largely the one the Morris family knew, with its Manor Farm, Home Farm, parish church, cottages, and pub, set among flat fields bordering the River Thames.

The east front of Kelmscott Manor; the old kitchen to the left of the porch, the old hall to the right.

Morris took great interest in Kelmscott Manor's history and its long connection to the working landscape, an interest continued by the Society of Antiquaries of London today.

In itself, Kelmscott Manor is in many ways unremarkable, a typical example of a gabled Oxfordshire farmhouse or small manor, with steep stone-tiled roofs and mullioned windows. An important farmhouse in the village, originally called Lower House or Lower House Farm, it apparently became known as the 'Manor' only when farmer-freeholder James Turner acquired land with a 'lord of the manor' title, in 1864. But it was the simplicity and ordinariness of the house that appealed to Morris; he felt it spoke of working lives and rural crafts, a world away from the distanced elegance of Georgian country seats like his childhood home, Woodford Hall in Essex; and different too from the turmoil and inhumanity of the cities of the Victorian industrial age.

The architecture of Kelmscott Manor is also woven into Morris's best-selling novel *News from Nowhere, or An Epoch of Rest* (1890), where an old stone house, a clear portrait of the actual Kelmscott Manor, stands at the end of a journey that explores utopian ideals within a post-industrial world. Morris imbued its simple architecture with profound values and regarded the care of such buildings as a social good. The book describes a 'many-gabled old house built by the simple country-folk of the long-past times, regardless of all the turmoil that was going on in cities and courts'. In the novelised manor house, simplicity is key: 'Everywhere there was but little furniture, and that only the most necessary, and of the simplest forms. The extravagant love of ornament... seemed here to have given place to the feeling that the house itself and its associations was the ornament of the country life amidst which it had been left stranded from old times'.

The frontispiece to the 1892 Kelmscott Press edition - drawn by Charles March Gere, engraved by W. H. Hooper - shows a view of Kelmscott Manor from the gate, with the text: 'This is the picture of the old house by the Thames to which the people of this story went'. Kelmscott Manor was both an 'Earthly paradise' and a home almost grown from the earth; a house put together without a 'grand office-architect', by builders 'traditionally acquainted with the best means of using wood and stone'.

The house played an important part in his family's creative life and many writers, artists and thinkers passed through its doors – and still do. Everyone has their own view of the house and its influence. In his 1928 biography of Rossetti, the novelist Evelyn Waugh conjured up a telling but unexpected image of Morris enjoying the thick walls and small rooms of Kelmscott Manor: 'Like some amiable mole, 'Topsy' Morris was happiest when his tawny form was curled up within these thick walls. They alone remained unchanged in Utopia, born of the earth and the native rightness of man'. Above all, Kelmscott Manor made Morris think deeply about the important things in life and the need to envisage a better future for Society.

It was certainly always a welcoming place. Its spirit is summed up in Morris's postscript to his printer Emery Walker before a visit in August 1888: 'P.S. As everybody may be out when you come look under the mat and you will find the house key. Enter and be happy.'

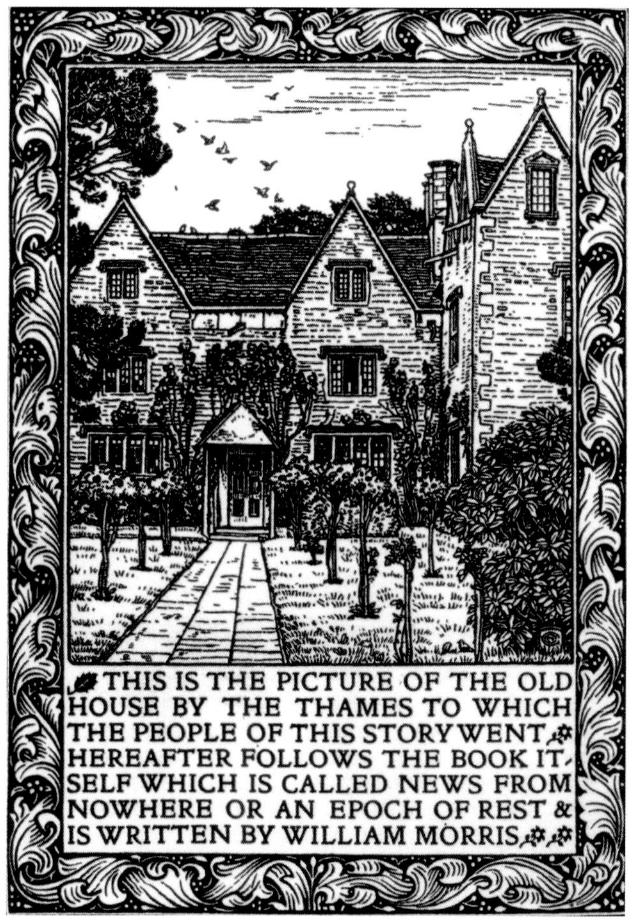

News from Nowhere frontispiece of the 1892 Kelmscott Press edition, drawn by Charles March Gere and engraved by W.H.Hooper.

FLOOR PLANS

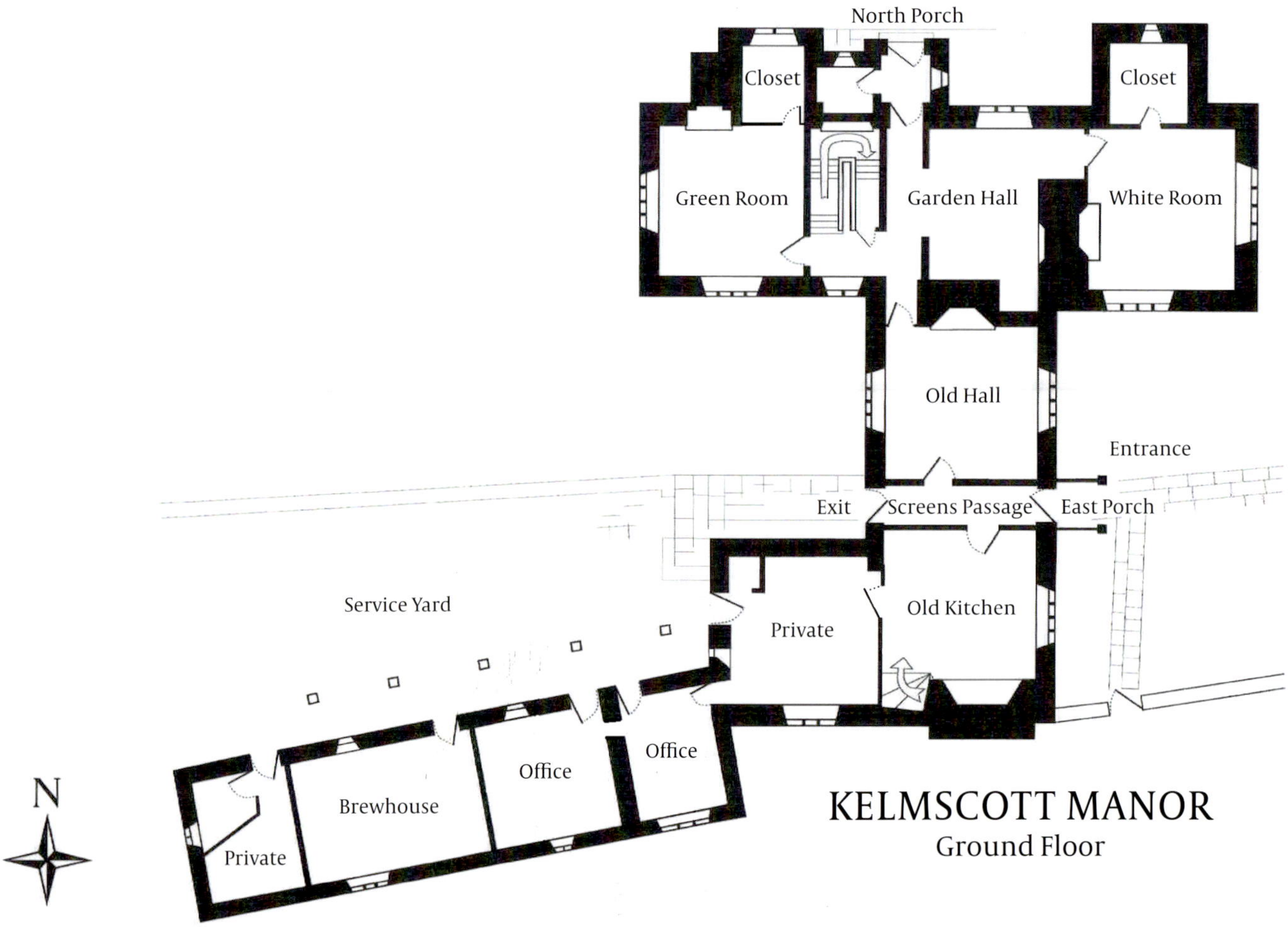

The Old Hall

The White Room

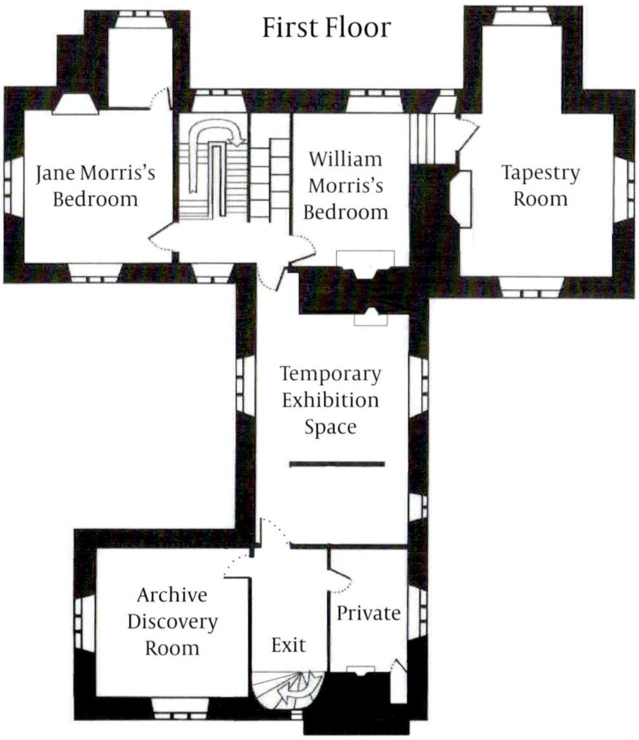

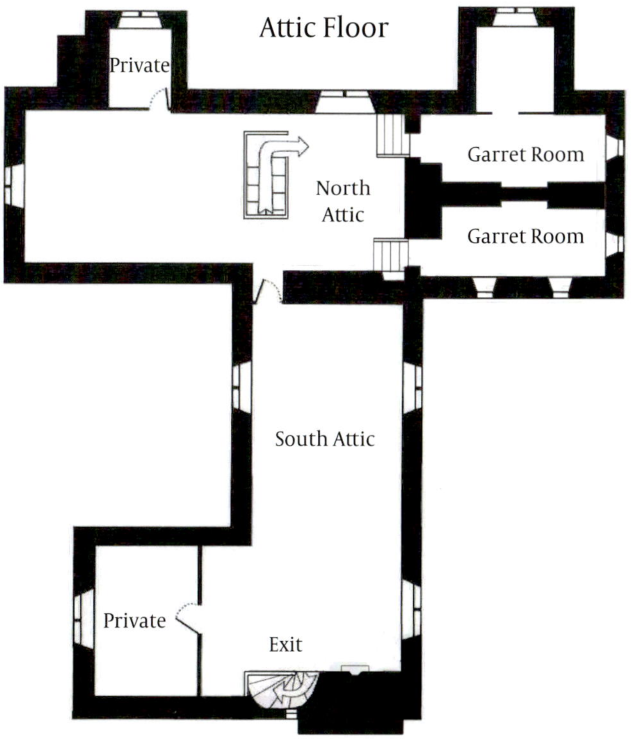

William Morris's Bedroom

The South Attic

TIMELINE

c.1600	Kelmscott Manor (then Lower House) built for farmer Thomas Turner (who inherited in 1594 and died in 1610)
1611	Inventory of the house taken, giving evidence of room names
1665	Turner's grandson, also Thomas, granted a coat of arms
c.1665-1670	builds new wing and remodels the old house with larger gables and windows
c.1728	The house divided into two dwellings; the southern end let to tenants
1734	Will of one George Turner, listing room names
1793	Enclosure of land at Kelmscott, changing the character of farming
1830s	The house returned to a single dwelling for Charles and Martha Turner
1834	William Morris born at Elm House, Walthamstow
1839	Jane Burden born in Oxford
1840	Morris's family move to Woodford Hall, Essex
1847	Morris's father dies, family move to Water House, Walthamstow, now the William Morris Gallery
1853	Morris enters Exeter College, Oxford, as an undergraduate
1857	Rossetti, Morris, Burne-Jones work together on decorating the Debating Chamber of the Oxford Union
1859	William Morris and Jane Burden marry
1859-60	Red House designed by Philip Webb for William and Jane Morris
1860-65	Morrises living at Red House, Kent (near Bexleyheath)
1861	Jenny Morris born
1861	Founding of 'the Firm' – Morris, Marshall, Faulkner & Company
1862	May Morris born
1864	James Turner buys land with manorial title, house renamed Kelmscott Manor
1868-1870	Morris publishes epic poem *The Earthly Paradise*
1869	James Turner dies and leaves Kelmscott Manor to nephew Charles Hobbs
1871	William Morris and Dante Gabriel Rossetti take a joint lease on Kelmscott Manor
1871	Morris travels to Iceland leaving Rossetti with Jane and the children at Kelmscott Manor for the summer
1874	Rossetti leaves Kelmscott Manor. Morris renews shared lease with his publisher Frederick Ellis (until 1884)
1875	Morris takes over 'the Firm', now renamed Morris & Company
1877	Morris co-founds the Society for the Protection of Ancient Buildings (SPAB) with Philip Webb

1878	Morris leases 'The Retreat' 26 Upper Mall, Hammersmith, renaming it Kelmscott House
1884	Morris founds the Socialist League
1890	Morris publishes *News from Nowhere*
1891	Morris founds the Kelmscott Press for fine art printing
1896	Morris dies
1899	J. W. Mackail publishes *Life of William Morris*
1902	Memorial Cottages completed at Kelmscott - designed by Philip Webb for Jane Morris, in memory of William Morris
1907	May Morris founds the Women's Guild of Art
1913	The freehold of Kelmscott Manor (leased since 1873) acquired by trustees on behalf of Jane Morris
1914	Jane Morris dies
1914	Manor Cottages at Kelmscott designed by Ernest Gimson in memory of Jane
1917	Mary Lobb arrives in Kelmscott and becomes May Morris's companion
1923	May Morris moves permanently to Kelmscott Manor
1934	Morris Memorial Hall opened by George Bernard Shaw
1935	Jenny Morris dies
1938	May Morris dies, bequeaths Kelmscott Manor to the University of Oxford
1939	Sale of some contents, other than those bequeathed to Oxford with the house: minor alterations to the house under architect T. G. Davidson
1962	University of Oxford gives up the house and it passes to residuary legatee, the Society of Antiquaries of London
1964-67	Major repair programme under Peter Locke of Donald Insall Architects; includes division for a resident tenant, and a new north porch
1967	Society of Antiquaries of London acquires freehold of farm buildings associated with Manor and opens Kelmscott to public
1993-94	Garden restored and re-designed by Landscape Architects, Colvin and Moggridge
2019-2022	Major programme of repairs and re-presentation carried out by Architecton for The Society of Antiquaries of London, with support of the National Heritage Lottery Fund and other benefactors

WILLIAM MORRIS

'The past . . . is living in us, and will be alive in the future which we are now helping to make'.

William Morris, 'The Lesser Arts', 1877.

William Morris (1834-1896) once described himself as 'an artist, and a literary man, pretty well-known'. He is today especially associated with the Arts and Crafts movement which developed under his influence, but also known for his work as a poet, artist, textile and wallpaper designer, novelist, printer, translator, conservationist, and socialist activist. In her 1994 biography, Fiona MacCarthy wrote of Morris's 'highly original, painfully heroic progress through life', calling him 'the great artist-craftsman of his period' and at the same time 'a passionate social reformer, an early environmentalist, an educationalist and would-be feminist'.

Morris was indefatigable and idiosyncratic, a prolific poet and writer, designer and craftsman, creative idealist and, later in life, a champion of the working classes and scourge of British imperialism in Africa and elsewhere. Some contemporaries found him 'tempestuous and exacting company', but MacCarthy says he 'knew a great deal but stayed peculiarly innocent'. He could be generous to a fault and was a loyal and often fun-loving friend. He was a doting father to his daughters, with the long-term illness of one of them inspiring him to even greater love, and also devoted to his wife Jane. Although their marriage was complex, even unsuccessful in some terms, there was also a deep and lasting bond.

Morris was born into a wealthy family living in Walthamstow, Essex (his father was a successful financier who invested, shortly before his death, in Devon copper mines, which made his children very well off). Inspired by chivalric history from childhood, Morris came under the influence of the medievalist Gothic Revival movement at the University of Oxford, where he was an undergraduate in 1853-55. He planned on becoming a clergyman, thought of being a painter, and worked briefly in the office of Gothic Revival architect G. E Street, where the senior clerk was Philip Webb (1831-1915), who would become one of William Morris's closest friends and collaborators. However, by 1868, Morris had achieved national fame as a poet and it was for poetry that he was most widely known in his lifetime, rather than for the Morris & Co. designs that are so widely recognisable today.

Morris's closest friend from Oxford was Edward Burne-Jones (1833-98), with whom he shared lodgings in London after university. In 1857, they both worked on the decoration of the university's Union Debating Chamber, under the direction of Dante Gabriel Rossetti, an established poet and painter, and co-founder of the Pre-Raphaelite Brotherhood. At the theatre one evening, Rossetti and Burne-Jones spotted Jane Burden in the audience, an Oxford stableman's daughter of unusual beauty, and asked her to model for the mural. Morris fell deeply in love with Jane, marrying her in 1859 and making her his companion and collaborator, especially in the fitting out of Red House, near Bexleyheath, designed by Philip Webb.

The Morrises lived at Red House (then in the rural hamlet of Upton, Kent), from 1859 to 1865. Built of red brick in a simplified Gothic Revival style, the real excitement of Red House was the interiors. Here, the Morrises and friends – Burne-Jones and his wife Georgiana ('Georgie'), Rossetti, Elizabeth ('Lizzie') Siddal and Charles Faulkner – decorated walls, ceilings and furniture using subjects part-conjured from medieval manuscripts and rooted in idealistic visions of earthly love. The difficulty of finding the right furnishings led them to design and make their own, which in turn inspired them to set up Morris, Marshall, Faulkner & Co. to produce furniture and furnishings, including stained-glass.

William Morris, 1874, by Frederick Hollyer.

Woodcut of William Morris by R Bryden.

Women carpet weavers at the Morris & Co. Merton Abbey works.

In late 1865, the Morrises left Red House to live principally over the Firm's business premises in Queen Square, London. In May 1871, Morris wrote to Charles Faulkner: 'I have been looking about for a house for the wife and kids, and whither do you guess my eye is turned now? Kelmscott, a little village, about two miles above Radcott Bridge – a heaven on earth; an old stone Elizabethan house like Water Eaton, and such a garden! close down on the river, a boat house and all things handy. I am going down there again on Saturday with Rossetti and my wife: Rossetti because he thinks of sharing it with us if the thing like looks likely'.

So, with Rossetti as co-tenant, they leased Kelmscott Manor from Charles Hobbs, nephew of the last Turner resident, for whose family it had been built. May Morris, who was nine in 1871, recalled a first summer 'basking by our gentle uneventful Thames'. As a country retreat, it was mostly used to provide a healthy summer environment for Jane and the children, and the shape and texture of the building set the tone over any elaboration of ornament.

Rossetti departed in 1874. In 1875, Morris took over sole control of the firm, now renamed Morris & Company. He had a talent for business and designed many of his best-known wallpapers and textiles while at Kelmscott Manor. The family left their London home at Queen

Rossetti's sketch of Morris reading and fishing at Kelmscott, 1871.

Square, initially for Horrington House in Chiswick, which Morris described as 'a VERY little house with a pretty garden'. In 1877, they moved to 'The Retreat', a roomy Georgian house in Hammersmith, and Morris re-named this Kelmscott House in homage to his country home. Morris's delight in Kelmscott Manor influenced the increasing interest of the Arts and Crafts movement in the Cotswolds, illustrated by the relocation of designers such as Ernest Gimson and C. R. Ashbee to the area.

Morris's epic poem *The Earthly Paradise* (1868-1870), and his novels *A Dream of John Ball* (1888), *News from Nowhere* (1890), and The *Well at the World's End* (1896) were widely read – he was a hugely popular writer in his lifetime, and his poetry was talked of as reviving the magic of Chaucer. In the late 1860s, Morris studied Icelandic under the guidance of Eiríkr Magnússon. He travelled with him to Iceland in 1871, and subsequently their joint English translations of Icelandic Sagas were published.

During the 1880s, having been a Liberal on the radical wing of the party, Morris became increasingly concerned with social inequality and the de-humanising conditions of the industrial working-classes and took a more public role in politics. Espousing Marxist views, he declared that he had crossed 'the river of fire' aged 49 and become a committed revolutionary Socialist, identifying as a Communist. After joining the Social Democratic Federation (SDF), Morris formed the Socialist League, interweaving his own brand of compassionate Socialism with Romantic anti-industrialism. He described it himself as 'practical socialism' rooted in the idea that 'harm to one would mean harm to all'.

In a speech to a Glasgow audience, Morris said: 'I have never known what I fear many of you unfortunately have known, actual poverty – the pain of to-day's hunger and cold, and the fear of tomorrow's, or the dread of a master's voice, or the hopeless despair of unemployment. I have, I truly believe, lived as happy a life as anyone could wish to live, save for the misery of seeing so much cruel wrong and needless suffering around me. Yet I am no more entitled to that happiness than any of my fellows'.

Whilst his architect friend, Philip Webb, and his daughters shared his political views, Jane did not

Water House, Walthamstow, William Morris's parents' home (now the William Morris Gallery).

Red House, near Upton in Kent (near Bexleyheath) built in 1859-60, designed by Philp Webb for William and Jane Morris (now National Trust).

share all of them, nor did the Burne-Joneses or Sydney Cockerell, Morris's secretary at the Kelmscott Press, and many of Morris's obituarists tended to play them down. However, writings such as *News from Nowhere* were influential on a generation of post-First World War Socialist activists and thinkers. Writing to May Morris in the 1930s, the economist Harold Laski said: 'You can be very sure that among at least the Socialists of my generation your father remains a constant and abiding inspiration', and Clement Attlee, Britain's post-war Labour prime minister, always had a portrait of Morris in his study and spoke of how Morris was more important to him than Marx; Labour politician Barbara Castle said that Morris's political poetry had charged her vision of Socialist fulfilment.

Increasingly incensed by the damage caused by over-enthusiastic building 'restoration' (especially of parish churches), Morris and Webb founded in 1877 the Society for the Protection of Ancient Buildings (S.P.A.B., nick-named 'Anti-Scrape'), for which Webb, with Morris and others, wrote a manifesto which has profoundly informed the evolution of conservation philosophy and practice in the UK and around the world. They wrote of the need to 'keep a watch on old monuments', as 'ancient buildings are ... sacred monuments of the nation's growth and hope'. Morris's passionate championing of handicraft, materials and simple, vernacular architectural forms influenced architectural development at the time, as designers moving away from the full Gothic Revival mode towards something plainer and less overtly historicist. It also influenced the following generation's 'Arts and Crafts' idealism, notably in the field of domestic architecture.

Morris's energy was relentless; as he lay dying, one of his physicians diagnosed his disease as 'simply being William Morris and having done more work than most ten men'. Marxist historian E. P. Thompson considered him simply 'one of those men whom history will never overtake'. His legacy is vast and diffuse and, once discovered, he tends to inspire people in multiple areas of endeavour.

Kelmscott Manor remains the ideal place to discover him, and to explore the inspiration he found in old architecture and the English countryside. As his daughter May Morris wrote, it was 'our dear riverside home, the home of his dreams'.

Morris and the Hammersmith Socialist League, c.1884.
Morris, standing second row, just to the right of the banner.

Kelmscott House, Hammersmith, William and Jane Morris's London home, from 1878.

JANE MORRIS AND KELMSCOTT MANOR

Jane Morris, posed by Rossetti, and photographed by John Parsons, 1865.

As an outstanding embroiderer, Jane ('Janey') Morris (1839-1914) – Jane Burden - played an important part in the evolution of the aesthetic of Red House and the firm that became Morris & Company. However, she is still probably best known as a model for the Pre-Raphaelite artists, especially Rossetti and Morris. Tall and lean, she clearly had a strong presence, and often wore medieval-inspired dress. After meeting her in 1869, the novelist Henry James wrote of 'an apparition of fearful and wonderful intensity' and 'a figure cut out of a missal', a reaction shaped by his familiarity with her in paintings before he met her in person.

Jane's father Robert Burden was a stable-hand at a Livery Stables in Oxford, and her mother Ann (née Maizey) probably worked in service or as a laundress. Both were from rural labouring families - her mother from Alvescot and her father from Stanton Harcourt. Jane herself grew up in cramped housing in Oxford, in an alleyway off St Helen's Passage, near New College. She was most likely put into service at fourteen. Jane had three siblings: brother William became a college messenger; one sister, Mary Ann,

A copy by Charles Fairfax Murray of *Water Willow* by Dante Gabriel Rossetti, 1871. This shows Jane Morris, the River Thames, and, in the top left hand, the gabled form of Kelmscott Manor.

died from tuberculosis at only fourteen in 1849, while her younger sister Elizabeth ('Bessie') later also had a career as a noted embroiderer.

With her unusual height, soulful eyes, dark wavy hair and sensuous mouth, Jane was not a conventional Victorian beauty. However, when she was seventeen her striking features were spotted by Rossetti and Burne-Jones in a theatre audience. She was what the pre-Raphaelite artists called a 'stunner', embodying a vision of womanhood from medieval Romance. Rossetti was already then engaged to working-class artist and model Elizabeth Siddal, whom he married in 1861, and while Rossetti painted Jane as Queen Guinevere in the Oxford Union Debating Chamber scheme, it was Morris who fell in love with her and proposed.

In the class-conscious Victorian era, Jane's marriage was socially transformative. She was intelligent and graceful, and the wealthy young Morris may have arranged for her to spend time studying, so that she could acquire the accomplishments of women of his own class. Her abilities as a letter writer are clear from correspondences with Webb and Rosalind Howard, later Countess of Carlisle. After her marriage, she

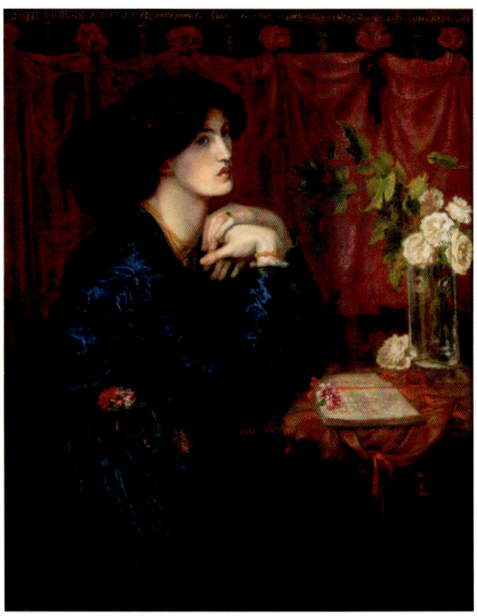

The Blue Silk Dress, Rossetti, 1868.

Jane Morris, and her daughters, May (left) and Jenny (right) with Ada Peerless, Jenny's nurse, at Kelmscott Manor in 1902.

spoke French and later Italian, and played the piano. Some contemporaries thought her 'queenly', and some have suggested her progress through society may have inspired the Morrises' friend George Bernard Shaw to write his play *Pygmalion* (the basis for the musical film *My Fair Lady*).

The Morrises' two daughters, Jenny and May were born at Red House, where love is a major theme of the decoration. Morris's painting of Jane as *La Belle Iseult*, 1858, (now in the Tate Gallery) captures an image of her as the radiant focus for earthly love. Jane embroidered wall-hangings for Red House and when the Morrises moved to Queen Square, London, in 1865, she took charge of a group of women, including her sister Elizabeth, to create ecclesiastical and domestic needlework for Morris, Marshall, Faulkner & Co. She later recalled: 'we were making experiments in silk and gold wools afterwards to bloom into altar cloths'.

Jane's marriage has been the subject of much speculation. Although it is clear that in later years there was strong mutual devotion, how much she loved Morris in those early years is less certain. Many years after the death of Elizabeth Siddal in 1862, there was a romantic liaison with Rossetti, which began in the later 1860s, and lasted until 1875. This may well have prompted the joint lease of Kelmscott Manor by Morris and Rossetti, with its remote location chosen to avoid scandal. Jane sat for a series of Rossetti portraits, often designing and making the costumes for them. Believing that 'fellowship is life', Morris himself found emotional rewards in close friendships, including with the embroiderer and artist Aglaia Coronio, and his 'spiritual affinity', Georgiana Burne-Jones. Jane was certainly deeply fond of Kelmscott Manor and the way of life they developed there when in retreat from London, writing of the summer in 1893, 'we have tea out of doors most days'.

Jane supported Morris's work with the Firm and with SPAB, and enjoyed the companionable life of Kelmscott Manor, but did not entirely share his idealistic socialism, retaining her own allegiance to the radical wing of the Liberal party. After Morris's death, she asked Webb to design cottages as a memorial, saying: 'you know how much cottages are needed for labourers in this countryside'. Alluding to Red House, Webb replied: 'Almost the very first building I set up was for you, and the very last, if I can so make it, will also be for you'. The Memorial Cottages were completed in 1902. In 1904, Jane also started a 'little Reading Room in one of my cottages' for local villagers, which she thought 'a great success'.

Jane left Kelmscott House, Hammersmith, after Morris's death, and transferred many furnishings to Kelmscott Manor. Jane and her daughters continued to value the Manor as a home and retreat. Jane's health was often frail, and Jenny was increasingly ill over the years. The freehold of the Manor was acquired by family trustees in 1913, shortly before Jane died in January 1914, aged 74, when the property was inherited by her daughter May.

ROSSETTI

The presence of poet and painter Dante Gabriel Rossetti (1828-1882) is crucial to the story of the Morrises' early association with Kelmscott Manor – and whether Morris would have followed the same path without Rossetti's early friendship is an interesting question. Rossetti, who was already romantically involved with Jane, shared the lease of the house with them. In July 1871, Morris went to Iceland, leaving Rossetti there with Jane and the children. This could be read as an act of coldness, or, perhaps more likely, one of generosity and forbearance, particularly towards Jane, as he appears to have hoped to protect her reputation from scandalous gossip.

Rossetti's father was an Italian political refugee, poet, and authority on the thirteenth-century Italian poet Dante; his mother, a teacher, was the sister of Lord Byron's Dr Polidori. Rossetti studied at the Royal Academy Schools in the 1840s, and at the studio of Ford Madox Brown. He shared a studio with William Holman Hunt, and in 1848, Rossetti, Hunt and John Everett Millais founded the 'Pre-Raphaelite Brotherhood', with William Michael Rossetti (Dante Gabriel's Rossetti's brother), James Collinson, Frederic George Stephens, and Thomas Woolner, championing 'truth to nature' in opposition to the formal classicism of the Academy.

In 1850, he was exhibiting as a painter while editing the Brotherhood's magazine *The Germ*, his poems and paintings infused with idealistic views of the medieval world. He became close to the painter Elizabeth ('Lizzie') Siddal – around 1849, but they married only in 1860. His painting *Ecce Ancilla Domini!* - using his sister Christina Rossetti, the poet, as his model - was widely disdained when first shown in April 1850 but is now regarded as one of the finest pre-Raphaelite artworks. Later works were also criticised as decadent, with even Rossetti's poetry attacked as being of 'the Fleshly' school.

By 1854, Rossetti was a friend of art critic John Ruskin, and he later befriended Edward Burne-Jones and William Morris, and encouraged them in their artistic ambitions. In 1857, Ruskin was instrumental in commissioning artists to decorate the new Debating Chamber of the Oxford Union, and Rossetti took six assistants, including Burne-Jones and Morris. One assistant recalled that Rossetti was in his element, 'humorous, witty and captivating . . . the sun round whom we revolved'.

Although Morris married Jane, she became Rossetti's most important model, with one of his finest paintings of her, *The Blue Silk Dress*, 1868, now hanging at Kelmscott Manor (illus p.52 & 77). Rossetti and Elizabeth Siddal helped in the decoration of Red House, and he was a founding partner in Morris, Marshall, Faulkner, and Co. In 1862, Elizabeth Siddal had died, after which Rossetti suffered bouts of depression and insomnia, with episodes of paranoia, while living alone in Chelsea. He became co-tenant of Kelmscott Manor with Morris, hoping it would improve his health. He lived there for long periods between 1871 and 1874, bringing furniture and paintings to the house, some of which remain today. Initially, he loved the peace of the Manor, the landscape and village, and going on 'splendid riverside walks'.

Rossetti was fond of the Morris children and, in 1871, he drew their portraits in pastel (see illus p.27). During the summer, he and Jane spent time in the Panelled (or White) Room and the Tapestry Room, with Rossetti drawing or reading aloud from Scott, Pepys and Boswell. His 1871 *Water Willow* portrait of Jane shows the house and riverscape, and a faithful copy, made in 1893, remains in the house.

In 1872, Rossetti spent the severe winter at Kelmscott Manor, without the Morrises; and in the summer of 1873, he wrote: 'I have done nothing but my daily painting all my time here'. He worked on *Proserpine and La Ghirlandata* before leaving Kelmscott in 1874, having become - according to his brother William - 'overstrained and fanciful' as his health continued to decline. Rossetti's *Ballads and Sonnets* (1881) expand on his sonnet sequence 'The House of Life' and touch on struggles with guilty love and sensuality. This too was censured in his lifetime, but its frankness and honesty about human desire and sexuality have been admired by later generations.

Dante Gabriel Rossetti, photographed by Lewis Carroll.

MAY AND JENNY MORRIS, DAUGHTERS OF WILLIAM AND JANE

May Morris (1862-1938), a talented designer-embroiderer and historian of embroidery, was a leading figure in the Arts and Crafts Movement. She spent the happiest parts of her childhood at Kelmscott Manor both indoors and outdoors. She later recalled that: 'we were never really town birds; country life was always the natural and happy thing'. She drew and painted the house with love and devotion; and explored every part of it and its grounds with her father and sister. She remembered 'romping and skirmishing in the garrets', and she loved 'roof riding': one time, she got stuck, and 'old Philip the gardener' was sent 'post haste for the longest ladders the village possessed'.

In her later years, May lived at Kelmscott more permanently than her parents, and actively planned how the house could be preserved as a memorial to her father. She bequeathed it to the University of Oxford in 1938, having chosen the furniture and artworks that should remain with the house. She should perhaps be thought of as the first curator, determined that Kelmscott Manor should remain a place of reference and resource for people inspired by her father's writings, work and values.

From 1914 to 1923, May had a house at 8, Hammersmith Terrace in London, but she spent long periods at the Manor during the First World War moving there for good in 1923. She commissioned a second pair of memorial cottages, from the architect Ernest Gimson, after her mother died in 1914 and led a campaign to build a village hall in William Morris's memory, wanting residents to feel involved in this tribute to their 'friend and champion'. Also designed by Gimson, the Memorial Hall was only completed in 1938, with the opening ceremony being carried out by May's former lover, the playwright, George Bernard Shaw. The hall was crowded and Ramsay MacDonald, just elected Prime Minister, arrived unannounced and was almost unable to get into the ceremony.

May was never a distant figure – one villager described her as a 'very nice, homely lady' - and she devoted herself to the welfare of the village's working families, running a soup kitchen for local children, founding one of the first women's institutes in the country and organising lectures, concerts, folk-dancing and singing lessons.

May also edited her father's *Collected Works* into a monumental 24 volumes, but she was far more than

Jenny Morris, 1871, by Rossetti.

May Morris, 1871, by Rossetti.

May Morris weaving in the Green Room, before 1921, behind her can be seen the *Kennet* chintz.

just a keeper of paternal memory. Brought up as a maker, she excelled in the design and execution of needlework, wallpaper design and jewellery-making. There are examples of her jewellery in both the National Museum of Wales and the Victoria and Albert Museum, London. She learnt embroidery from her mother and aunt at an early age, and from 1881 she studied design at the National Art Training School - precursor to the Royal College of Art - where she took embroidery as her special subject.

At twenty-three, in 1885, May became director of Morris & Co.'s embroidery department, but left after her father's death to become a freelance designer and practitioner, and to teach embroidery at colleges in London, Birmingham and Leicester. As a counterpart of the then all-male Art Workers Guild, she founded the Women's Guild of Arts in 1907.

May had married Henry Halliday Sparling in 1890, but the marriage was not a success and they divorced in 1899. She never remarried. From 1917, however, she had the companionship of Mary Lobb, who arrived in the village from the West Country as a land girl and made friends with May. Mary then worked at Kelmscott Manor as a gardener-come-groom and soon became her companion, in effect a part of the family. One visitor remembered 'her shining eyes, red cheeks, enthusiasm', describing her as loving ponies and the land, living a life she 'never wanted to leave'.

She was tough too: Bernard Shaw described her as someone 'strong enough to take me by the scruff of the neck and pitch me neck and crop out of the curtilage'. The poet John Betjeman retained a warm impression of her, remembering especially her 'ample laughter'.

Many assumed, then as now, that May and Mary had a romantic relationship, which is possible. There is no clear documentary evidence, and following the First World War, which left so many widows, it was not at all uncommon for women to share homes for life. They were certainly a devoted pair, and travelled together as far as Iceland, while back at Kelmscott, they ran the property together, and were enthusiastic hands-on gardeners. Mary died in 1939, not long after May's death in 1938. Mary Lobb wrote to the Director of the V&A Museum in 1938, to say: 'William Morris could design embroideries, but he could not embroider, any way not as well as Miss Morris could, Mrs Morris could embroider but couldn't design, Miss Morris could and did both'.

May's older sister, Jenny (Jane) was born in 1861, also at Red House, near Bexleyheath. As children, the girls were close and shared the friendship of the Burne-Jones children. Jenny modelled for artists including Rossetti who described the

Jenny Morris in the White Room at Kelmscott Manor, 1878 in front of the 1660s chimneypiece, then still painted in marble effect (see illus p.53).

children in 1871 as 'dear little things . . . able to amuse themselves all day long'. Like her mother, aunt and sister, Jenny was skilled in embroidery; she was a clever, academic child who did well at a day school in Notting Hill and had hopes of studying at Cambridge or Oxford.

Sadly, she was diagnosed with epilepsy at the age of fifteen and left school. In the nineteenth century, this condition was regarded as a type of severe mental illness and sufferers were stigmatised. There was little in the way of treatment, except for dangerous and damaging Potassium Bromide. Jenny had to be under constant surveillance, and her health was a source of deep anxiety to her parents, with William perhaps seeming to be the more doting - but more often absent. Although Jane was considered by some as more distant, she once wrote to a friend that it was 'a dreadful grief for us all' and she was unceasing in her attention to Jenny's care.

A glimpse of Jenny's cleverness is suggested in 1878-79 when, in a lull in her illness, she created a magazine of stories and articles called *The Scribbler*, published fortnightly by the Morris and Burne-Jones children (a young Burne-Jones cousin called Rudyard Kipling was included in one issue). Jenny's condition fluctuated and, at times, she had to reside with a nurse-companion, but she remained a warm and well-regarded person and an active Socialist. By 1884, with her epilepsy worsening, Jenny went to live in Malvern under the supervision of a nurse. But she was often at Kelmscott Manor, enjoying its calm and quiet, with her nurse; in 1905 Jane wrote of her being well and 'so sweet and affectionate always to those about her'. Jane also wrote how Jenny, 'never wearies of this place – where she knows every tree and plant'.

Later, Jenny lived with a nurse in Somerset and when May wrote her will leaving Kelmscott Manor to the University of Oxford, as a country residence for some important office holder, she stipulated that should her sister survive her, Jenny would be entitled to spend a month a year there. In the event, Jenny died first, at the age of 74, in 1935. Jenny left money, possessions and her fathers' books to the Society of Antiquaries of London, long before they owned Kelmscott Manor. She also left May a further legacy to help to set up the Society of Antiquaries of London's William and Jane Morris Memorial Fund for the protection and restoration of ancient churches, which is still issuing grants for conservation of decorative or non-structural features.

May Morris and Mary Lobb in Wales in 1926.

Over the page: May Morris in the Tapestry Room at Kelmscott Manor, Mary Annie Sloane, 1912.

KELMSCOTT MANOR AND ITS BUILDINGS

Kelmscott Manor was built as a residence for a working farmer, and Morris loved the simple, handcrafted quality of the building and its outlying barns – including – 'the huge barn . . . alive with busy men and women' as May recalled. The construction of house and barns was carried out by local stonemasons, carpenters, and joiners; and Morris felt the use of locally quarried stone made the walls appear almost to have grown from the earth.

The core of Kelmscott Manor was built in about 1600, probably for yeoman farmer Thomas Turner, who inherited in 1594 and died in 1610. Stylistic analysis of the fireplaces suggests the date of around 1600. The Turners were a long-standing farming family who had lived and worked in the local area from the fifteenth century and remained one of the key families into the twentieth century. The original house was snug, with a modest U-shaped plan: the hall at the centre, kitchen and services to the south, the main staircase to the north, led to the principal chambers at the north end of the house on the first floor, with at least one parlour, the current Green Room, below.

The house was extended to the north east for another Thomas Turner (d.1685) in the later 1660s,

Left: The east front of Kelmscott Manor: the older part of the house was built c.1600.

Above: The north part, to the right, was added in the late 1660s, at which time the gables over the older part (to the left) were also raised.

and a two-storey bay was also added to the parlour range, providing closets on two floors. Thomas married Anna, daughter of Sir Thomas Faulcons, and was granted a coat of arms in 1665, which moved him more into the ranks of country 'gentry' - the hereditary landowners who dominated local (and national) politics and administration. His extension and smartening-up of the house appears to have followed quickly afterwards. At the same time as this work, the windows of the c.1600 house were very probably enlarged at this time, and the gables of the older house were also made larger and ornamented with copings and ball finials to match the new work. This was presumably to make better use of the first-floor attics for servants' accommodation.

The historic core of Kelmscott Manor is therefore still just one room deep, and was an essentially functional series of spaces in the medieval tradition, consisting of a single-storey hall and a kitchen, with rooms over and some attic spaces under the roofs. Then, as today, the front door leads into a 'screens passage' that divides the Old Hall, the communal room of the original farmhouse to the north, from the kitchen to the south – an arrangement which began to fall out of fashion from the early seventeenth century.

To the north of the Old Hall is the Garden Hall - which was the principal entrance during the Morrises' occupation - leading to the main staircase which dates to around 1600. The screens passage also leads

The north front of Kelmscott Manor, with the 1660s addition to the left.

directly through into the evocative service yard, west of the house. The southern side of this yard is formed of a single-storey range of seventeenth- or early eighteenth-century stone outbuildings, including a brew-house, with stone-tiled roofs – these were originally free-standing but were linked to the house in the nineteenth century.

Just beyond this is a handsome freestanding stone-walled privy with a pyramidal stone roof, probably of the 1660s, which looks a little like a garden temple.

As noted, in the later 1660s the north end of the house was remodelled and extended to the east to form the current tower-like, double-gabled block, with large mullioned and transomed windows to each floor on each face. At the top of each gables' face, of this later addition, is a single-light window in the attic level, and each of these is surmounted by a triangular pediment, a little Classical flourish on the otherwise traditional form.

In around 1728 the house was divided into two, and at least the service end tenanted out, but both parts were re-united for a member of the Turner family in the 1830s. The parlour on the north-east corner of the house was panelled in the early eighteenth century, possibly for one George Turner, and this room has long been known as the White Room (sometimes referred to as the Panelled Room). Minor works followed the arrival of the Morrises in 1871 and again

The gables of the west front seen across the service yard.

when the University of Oxford took over the house in 1939, but few major architectural alterations were made after the early eighteenth century until the major restoration carried out in the 1960s.

Kelmscott Manor's high walled garden enclosure adjoins a farmyard with two substantial, stone gabled barns and other outbuildings. The yard is bordered to the south by a man-made water channel, the Radcot Cut. Probably dating from the later seventeenth century, the barns were originally for crop storage and stock management, with a dovecot close to the house and a stable. The Threshing Barn, closest to the lane, has a handsome timber roof structure - of a type known as a triple-purlin collar with tie-beam; Morris greatly admired its traditional stone roof, a replacement for earlier thatch. The Stable Barn now houses the Tea Room.

During the 2019-2021 programme of works, a new single-storey thatched timber Learning Barn, designed by Architecton, was built on the axis of a lost cattle byre, and this recreates the earlier enclosed feeling of the yard. Slightly to the west – across the Tea Lawn - is a partly nineteenth-century, brick-and-stone granary building, now the Shop. Another timber-framed, seventeenth-century barn stands in the meadow (called the Home Mead by Morris), and an early seventeenth-century stone threshing barn lies to the north of the garden alongside the lane. Together with the manor house, they form an important group of faithfully preserved vernacular buildings.

The Tea Lawn between the tearoom barn and the granary was, in the late nineteenth century, the rickyard. May Morris sketched this filled with thatched ricks (haystacks), the construction of which was described by her father, in a letter to Georgiana Burne-Jones, in September 1881: 'the next morning the thatchers were putting the bright straw cap to the new rick: yesterday they were carrying the wheat in the field along our causeway and were stacking it in our yard: pretty as one sat in the Tapestry Room to see the loads coming in between the stone walls'.

The service courtyard and the west front of Kelmscott Manor, looking towards the north range.

THE GARDEN

The garden, divided by old clipped yew hedges, is quite unaffected & very pleasant, & looks in fact as if it were a part of the house, yet at least the clothes of it.

'Gossip about an Old House on the Upper Thames',
William Morris, 1895

Kelmscott Manor stands in a wider tapestry of agricultural landscape and spread-out village settlements, as well as its own patchwork of garden, yards and meadow. The front garden is enclosed by a stone wall, and to the north and west lie an orchard, flower garden and the wider area of meadow or 'home mead'.

The gardens were evidently important to Morris, who cherished the Manor's cottage-like qualities and closeness to nature. He had a special sensitivity to the relationship of house and its garden setting, feeling the architecture 'had grown up out of the soil' informed by 'some thin thread of tradition, a half-anxious sense of the delight of meadow and acre and wood and river . . .a certain amount of good sense'.

He drew inspiration from natural forms in his textile and wallpaper designs, although individual plants were often studied in the stylised illustrations in ancient herbals. According to May Morris, *Strawberry Thief* was directly inspired by Kelmscott Manor's garden and the famous *Willow Boughs* pattern was inspired by the presence of willows around house and fields, and overhanging the Thames, where he would fish from

Left: Trees and flowers frame views to and from the house.
Above: The north west corner of the house, seen from the garden.

a punt. May Morris later recalled walking along the Cut with her father, 'we were walking one day by our little stream that runs into the Thames, and my father pointed out the detail and variety of the leaf-forms, and soon afterwards this paper was done, a keenly-observed rendering of our willows that has embowered many a London living-room'.

When Morris found the house, he wrote to his friend Faulkner that it had 'such a garden!'. In 'Hopes and Fears for Art', 1882, he argued that a garden should 'look both orderly and rich, be well fenced from the outside world. It should by no means imitate either the wilfulness or the wildness of Nature, but should look like a thing never to be seen except near a house. It should, in fact, look like a part of the house'. Echoed in his 1895 essay 'Gossip about an Old House on the Upper Thames', this sentiment can be traced through the whole story of Arts and Crafts gardening. In *News from Nowhere*, he wrote of 'that delicious superabundance of small, well-tended gardens'.

The examples of Red House's garden enclosures set within orchards and Kelmscott Manor's abundant, part-enclosed gardens were both influential to the development of Arts and Crafts garden design. Morris's descriptions of imaginary gardens in his widely read poems also played a role. Arguably, the most obvious inspiration arose from the iconic view shown in the 1892 frontispiece of *News from Nowhere*. This seems to have defined the very idea of an English garden path approaching a rose-covered porch, in a gabled front.

Vegetable gardens appear in the bird's eye view of Kelmscott Manor, drawn by E. H. New in the 1890s. Jane Morris wrote to a friend, on July 30, 1893, that the 'garden is lovely and quite full of flowers and melons & cucumbers, we are thinking of trying vegetarianism but not till after your visit'. Jane loved flowers, and wrote

Standard roses line the path to the entrance on the east front.

View of Kelmscott Manor from the Old Barn, 1880s, watercolour by May Morris.

to Wilfrid Blunt, April 1, 1905: 'I am feeling stronger with the warmer weather, I can almost see flowers grow, cherry-blossom just bursting, and two rows of white lilies are starting up for blossom'. She had herself replanted the lilies and new rose the previous year.

The gardens were grassed over in the 1950s to reduce maintenance costs, but in the mid-1990s, the decision was taken to revive and restore them. Landscape architects Colvin and Moggridge reinstated some of the former areas of planting, using the evidence of old photographs and with an emphasis on flowers that appear in pre-Raphaelite paintings: hollyhocks and lilies, and trellises with climbing roses. They followed Morris's own dictum that 'On the whole, I think, the best and safest plan is to mix up your flowers, and rather eschew great masses of colour'. The Meadow, to the west, and orchard are maintained with long grass and wildflowers, with traditional trees such as crab apples, ash, willow, walnut and black poplar.

The front garden reflects the one in the famous 1892 frontispiece, with standard roses – including *Mary Rose, Heritage, Sir Edward Elgar* and *Countryman* – lining the path. The yew hedge on the east lawn was first clipped into the shape of dragon Fafnir from the Old Norse *Völsunga Saga* (as co-translated and published by Morris in 1870) although it was not originally as large. May Morris could recall her father trimming the hedge, 'cutting the dragon's hair'.

Hal Moggridge wrote in 1995 of the garden being re-made not as an exact restoration but 'to provide the visitor with a peaceful and satisfying inspiration from plants, comparable to that which Morris himself enjoyed when he was at Kelmscott'. Here in these well-tended gardens, visitors can easily feel the beauty of nature and historic architecture than inspired the Morrises, in both life and art.

E.H. New's view of Kelmscott Manor and its barns and gardens, as Morris knew them.

CAUGHT IN TIME: KELMSCOTT MANOR IN 1896 AND 1897, AS PHOTOGRAPHED BY FREDERICK H. EVANS

Kelmscott Manor: Front and Dove-Cot (1896)

The attic (1896)

The Tapestry Room (1897)

Jane Morris's bedroom (1896)

William Morris's Bedroom (1896)

TOUR OF THE HOUSE: ROOM-BY-ROOM

The introductory quotations are taken from Morris's 1895 essay, 'Gossip about an Old House on the Upper Thames'. As this has something of the character of a guided tour, it helps us imagine Morris, or perhaps his daughter May, as our guide.

Detail of the *Fruit* wallpaper with portrait of Jane Morris by Charles March Gere.

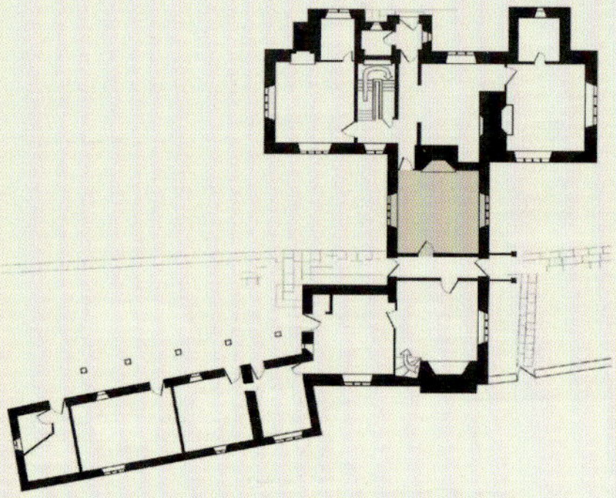

THE OLD HALL

'the whole room has a good deal the look of a particularly pleasant cabin at sea, were it not for the elms and the rooks on the west, and the green garden shrubs and blackbirds on the east. The room is really the heart of the Kelmscott house having been the parlour of the old house.'

At the centre of the house when it was built c.1600, the Old Hall was created as a multiple-use room for living, eating, and entertaining. A chamfered beam runs north-south across the ceiling and a screens passage – with broad elmwood planks set in narrow studs in the 'plank-and-muntin' method – separates the room from the kitchen, pantries, and sculleries, reducing draughts into the hall and screening the service rooms.

The stone chimney-surround dates from around 1600; during the Morrises' occupation however, this was concealed behind a later arrangement, which was itself surmounted by a Webb-designed timber chimneypiece that can be seen in old photographs. In 1871, Jane wrote to Webb about replacing the broken stone mantel-shelf she found in this room, saying: 'it would look well with tiles . . . They must be blue'. The original stone surround was rediscovered and revealed in the 1960s.

On his 1890s sketch plan of the house, Webb notes: 'Entrance is wood at present: it should be paved'. However, this seems to have been re-laid in wood block and only stone-flagged in the 1960s (indeed, stones taken from this room in the 1890s were laid in the passage and corridor at the foot of the stairs). The walls are hung with *Strawberry Thief* chintz, first printed in 1883, and probably in this room from 1890. May Morris believed her father to have been inspired to create this by watching thrushes in the garden – 'You can picture my Father going out early in the morning and watching rascally thrushes at work on the fruit-beds'. In 2021, the window-seats, shutters and doors were repainted in the dark green colour ('Brunswick Green') introduced by Morris but long since painted over. An interested visitor in 1896 described the room as 'painfully plain', but the Morrises loved its simplicity and used it as their principal dining room.

Left: The Old Hall, with the timber screens' passage behind.

Top: One of William Morris's own quill pens.

Middle: The Old Hall hearth of c1600, which was revealed during works in the 1960s.

Bottom: A detail of The *Strawberry Thief* chintz, first printed in 1883. Underneath is a piece of the original unfaded fabric from the collection for comparison.

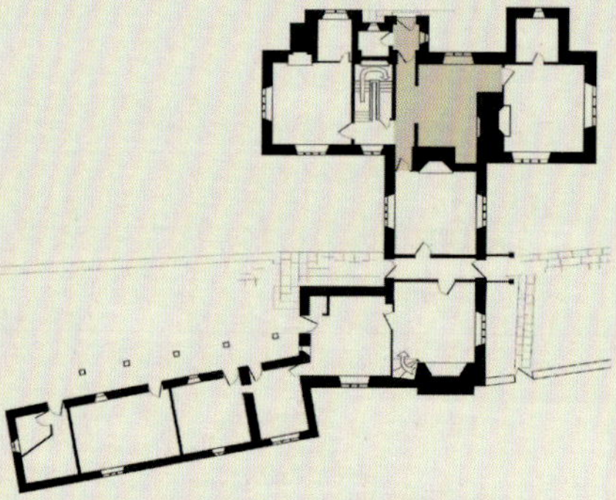

THE NORTH (OR GARDEN) HALL

Going under an arched opening in the yew hedge which makes a little garth about a low door in the middle of the north wall, one comes into a curious passage or lobby, a part of which is screened into a kind of pantry by wooden mullions which have once been glazed, and offer somewhat of a problem to the architect.

This was the principal entrance during the Morrises' occupation. The original purpose of this space is, however, uncertain; it may possibly have been some kind of store or private parlour behind the Old Hall. It has been subject to some changes over time: the oak screen mentioned by Morris was removed in 1939 and re-used on the first floor. It was then moved again to enclose this passage from the north door to the Old Hall in the 1960s, when the current north door was re-located on a slightly different alignment. The stone flags are probably the ones laid in this area by Morris, in 1895, and the dark green paint of the Morrises' original scheme was re-instated in 2021.

The screen is hung with the *Daisy* hanging. Designed by William Morris for Red House, it was embroidered on blue serge by Jane (see, p.73) with assistance from her sisters, who wrote of how they 'worked in bright colour in a simple rough way'. On the south wall is *If I Can* (1857), Morris's first attempt at embroidery, and his first attempt at woven tapestry (1879), which he called *Cabbage and Vine*, (see, p.78) hangs on the west wall. Together, these works evoke the early invention and industry of both Morrises, from which flowed so much else.

Top: The North Hall, also called the Garden Hall, part of the c.1600 house, but altered.

Middle: The Japanese chairs belonged to Rossetti.

Bottom: The textiles which hang here are important works of William and Jane Morris.

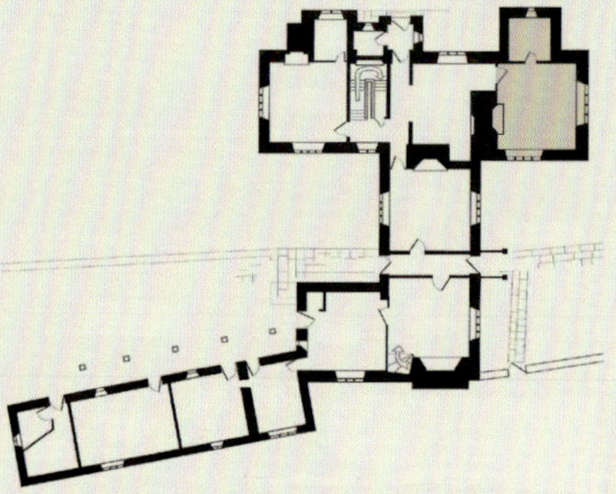

THE WHITE ROOM AND CHINA CLOSET

The said lobby leads into what was once the great parlour (the house is not great at all, remember) and is now panelled with pleasing George 1st panelling painted white: the chimney-piece is no doubt of the date of the building, and is of rude but rather amusing country work.

The White Room was called the 'Great Parlour' in 1734. It has a distinctive carved-stone chimneypiece which carries a cartouche painted with the arms granted to Thomas Turner in 1665, and the overmantel has a bolection-moulded frame between two fluted pilasters. In Morris's time, the chimneypiece was painted to resemble marble (see illus p.29), but this, probably a late seventeenth-century effect, was removed in the early 1900s.

The panelling is of a type known as 'raised and fielded', with a framed panel raised to the same plane as the frame and was inserted in the early eighteenth century. The floor of wood blocks was probably laid for Morris, and it appears from recent analysis that he – perhaps in conjunction with Rossetti – introduced the white scheme in the 1870s, as well as white linen curtains that added to the room's cooling atmosphere during the summer.

It was sometimes used as the schoolroom, with May Morris recalling how in 1871 in: 'those glowing August mornings we sat in the pleasant cool of the Panelled Room trying to learn things about Roman emperors and outside the wide mullioned windows the blackbirds were chuckling and feasting among the gooseberries: golden stacks were growing roof-high in the yard outside and the huge barn was alive with busy men and women. It was all too interesting: the Roman emperors were not to be endured for long and Mother became philosophical about my truancy'.

Along with Rossetti's portrait of Jane Morris in a blue silk dress, the early nineteenth-century square piano was in this room in 1895. The painted settle and robust Gothic Revival style round table were designed by Webb for Red House. Both were once at Kelmscott House in London, before being brought to Kelmscott Manor. Off this room is the China Closet, lit by the single opening of what was originally a six-light mullioned and transomed window. The shelves were especially designed for the space by Webb to display Morris's collection of Chinese, Japanese and Dutch blue-and-white china.

Left: The White Room was panelled in the 1730s, the *Blue Silk Dress*, 1868, is a portrait of Jane Morris by Rossetti.

Top: Painted settle by Philip Webb formally at Red House and Kelmscott House.

Middle: The stone chimneypiece was added in the 1660s. It was originally painted in marble effect (see illus p.29).

Bottom: The China Closet, with display shelves designed by Philip Webb.

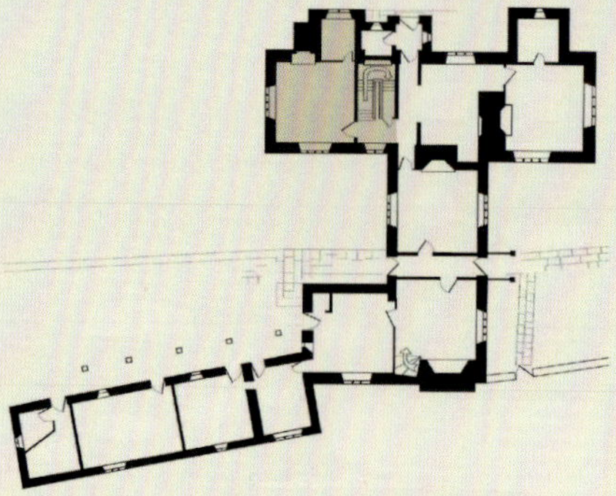

GREEN ROOM, STAIRS AND LANDING

'Going back to the little passage which leads to the lobby one comes to the staircase, of a common Elizabethan pattern with spherical knobs on the standards.'

The Green Room, just west of the foot of the stairs, was probably the 'Inner Parlour' named in the 1611 inventory. A fireplace was added in the late 1660s at the same time as the closet, which also had its own fireplace. In 1873, Jane wrote to Webb about her intention to add tiles of Morris's *Swan* and *Artichoke* patterns to the hearth in the Green Room. Missing tiles were replaced with *Sunflower* and *Snakehead* in the 1960s. The floor is now (after flood damage) in breathable lime-crete, scored to read as stone flags. Previously, stone flags had been laid for Morris (with advice from Webb) to replace the 'machine tiles' noted in Webb's 1895 plan.

Morris often threw himself into home improvement, and wrote of this room to Jane in 1892, saying: 'I got in such a mess down in the Green Room, and painted myself so much'. Paint analysis revealed the original, dark green ('Brunswick Green') and led to the 2021 re-painting of the woodwork. This includes the panelled overmantel designed by Webb, re-instated in 2021 after being stored in an outhouse since the 1960s. A closet screen has also been re-created, restoring the room to the proportions of the Morrises' period of occupation. Frederick H. Evans's 1896 photograph shows the room hung, as it is now, with Morris's *Kennet* chintz, designed in 1883.

This was also the favourite room of May Morris, when she was living full-time in the house from 1923 to 1938, and here she worked on her own projects while leaving other main rooms as a memorial to her father. In 1926, she writes of the *Kennet* chintz being 'much faded' and references a 'very worn' Turkey carpet from Red House. She also mentions a sofa from 'Queen Square with Wandle chintz cushions' as well as 'My Carved Chair from Hammersmith', reminding us of the way she curated this house with all its memories.

The handsome staircase is of a typical late-sixteenth/early seventeenth-century form with turned hourglass banisters, square newels with bulbous knobs and finials, and a drop pendant. In Morris's day this was probably painted the same dark green ('Brunswick Green') used elsewhere, but it was stripped and waxed after 1921. The rare sixteenth-century paintings of Lisbon (originally one painting but divided and framed separately by Rossetti) depict the Rua Nova des Mercadores, which was destroyed in the devastating 1755 earthquake; these were from Rossetti's collection. In 1926, there was a stair carpet of *Blue Flower* pattern, of which a fragment survives in the collection.

The elm staircase of c.1600.

The floor is in a breathable lime-crete, scored to read as stone flags.

Left: The Green Room, hung with *Kennet* chintz; the wooden screen to the right was inserted in 2021, to help recreate the effect of the orginal closet here. The chimneypiece is later 1660s, the overmantel was designed by Philip Webb and was re-installed here in 2021 having been stored in an outbuilding. It has been repainted in the original 'Brunswick Green'.

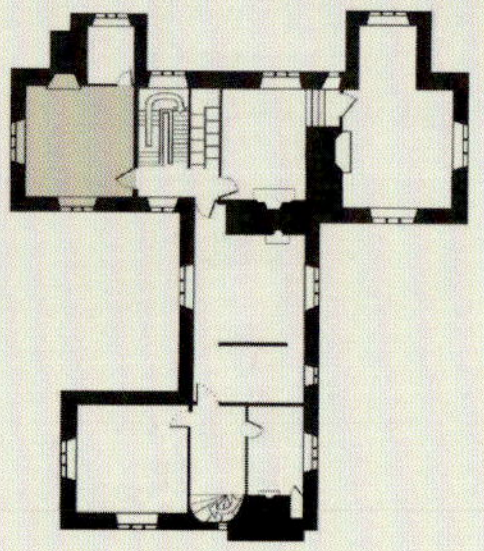

JANE MORRIS'S BEDROOM

The 1611 inventory refers to this room as 'Chamber over the Parlour'. The bed Jane slept in was a Morris family piece; May Morris records that it came from the family home and was the bed in which Morris was born, and was 'given to him by his mother on his coming to Kelmscott Manor'.

An 1896 photograph by Frederick H. Evans shows the room with *Fruit* (also called *Pomegranate*) wallpaper and distinctive *Small Stem* printed cotton bed hangings - the latter originally an 1829 design, but printed in the late 1860s for Morris, Marshall, Faulkner & Co., by Lancashire calico printer, Thomas Clarkson. The south window (against which the bed stood in 1896) had been blocked in the early eighteenth century, but was part re-opened before 1921, and the side lights unblocked by the University of Oxford in 1939-40. In the 1960s, the room was re-papered in the well-known *Willow Boughs* paper and the bed hung with matching drapes; in recent works, it has been rehung with a copy of the *Fruit* wallpaper, hand-printed (by Sanderson's) using the original blocks; and the bed re-upholstered (by A.T.Cronin Workshop Ltd) with hangings and valance, which replicate the lost originals.

In the 1960s, the nineteenth-century timber chimney surround was removed to reveal the Elizabethan stone fire-surround behind. The original closet partition survives (somewhat altered), and Jane used this divided area as her dressing room.

Jane Morris's bedroom has been re-hung in 2021 with hand-blocked wallpaper, *Fruit*, to return it to the character recorded in Frederick H. Evans 1896 photograph.

Top: The bed (in which William Morris had been born) has been rehung in *Small Stem*, an 1829 design printed by Thomas Clarkson for Morris, Marshall, Faulkner & Co.

Middle and bottom: The juxtaposition of patterned wallpaper and bed hangings is suggestive of the inspiration of Nature in the Morrises' visual culture.

William Morris's Bedroom also served as the approach to the Tapestry Room. The hand-blocked *Lily* wallpaper was hung here in 2021 to return the room to is character in Morris's lifetime.

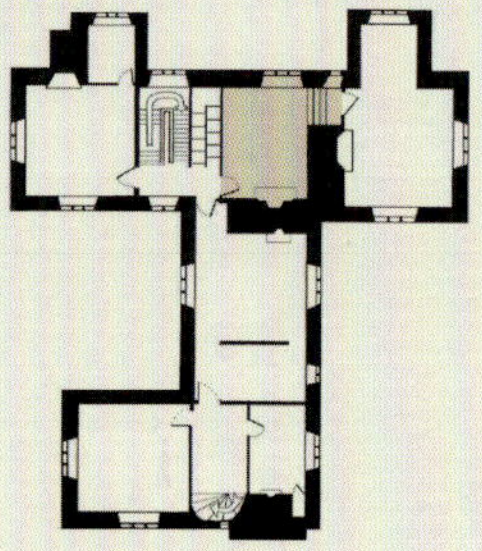

WILLIAM MORRIS'S BEDROOM

'On to the first floor which has the peculiarity of being without passages, so that you have to go from one room into another, to the confusion of some of our casual visitors, to whom a bed in the close neighbourhood of a sitting-room is dire impropriety.'

Called the 'Middle Chamber' in 1611, Morris's bedroom was something of a corridor, with steps leading to the Morrises' principal drawing room, the Tapestry Room. Morris referred to it as 'our present best bedroom' and seems to have relished it being the meeting place of original house and the seventeenth-century addition. He noted the room was the 'only north room' of the house' with a north facing window.

Morris wrote a poem honouring the comforts of his bed, which was probably made up in the 1840s from a mix of sixteenth- and seventeenth- century carved oak pieces:

The wind's on the wold
And the night is a-cold,
And Thames runs chill
'Twixt mead and hill.
But kind and dear
Is the old house here
And my heart is warm
'Midst winter's harm.
Rest then and rest,
And think of the best
'Twixt summer and spring,
When all birds sing
In the town of the tree,
And ye lie in me
And scarce dare move,
Lest earth and its love
Should fade away
Ere the full of the day.
I am old and have seen
Many things that have been;
Both grief and peace
And wane and increase
No tale I tell
Of ill or well,
But this I say:
Night treadeth on day,
And for worst or best
Right good is rest

These lines were embroidered in Gothic script on the pelmet and May also designed the hangings, which were embroidered by the women of the Morris & Co. embroidery department. The pattern followed *Trellis*, Morris's first wallpaper design - the latter was based on the rose trellises of the garden at Red House, with exotic birds drawn by Webb. Charles March Gere recalled Morris's habits on rising: 'He used to tumble out of bed, have his tub, slip into his blue shirt, and blue suit, thrust a brush – or maybe only his hands – through his curly hair and beard – all the work of a few moments – and was ready for the day's adventure'.

An old photograph shows a bolection-moulded timber chimneypiece, probably of the late nineteenth century date, as well as a late-nineteenth century iron grate. The timber surround was removed in the 1960s restoration - to reveal the stone fire surround of about 1600 - but was identified in the stores and has been refitted in 2021. Frederick H. Evans' 1896 photograph show *Lily* wallpaper (designed in 1874) on a blue-green background; this has been especially replicated, hand printed with the original blocks, by the present-day Morris & Co. (Sanderson's). The bookcase came from Kelmscott House in Hammersmith and was designed by Webb.

The bed hangings were designed by May Morris, and embroidered by the women of the Morris & Co embroidery department.

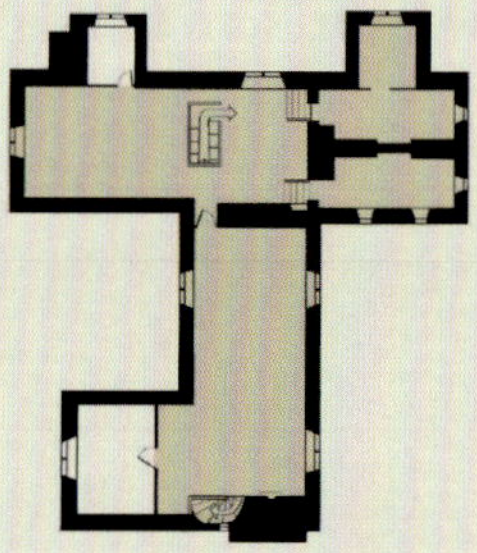

THE ATTICS

'we come to a newel stair-case, which comes up from the kitchen, and leads us up into the attics, i.e. the open roof under the slates; a very sturdy collar beam roof of elm often unsquared; it is most curiously divided under most of the smaller gables into little chambers where no doubt the hired field labourers, slept in old time: the bigger space is open and a fine place for children to play in.'

The attic rooms are in the roof space of the house and provide a chance to see and feel the structure of the building, as well as the repairs necessary to keep it sound. The timbers, mostly of elm, were extensively repaired in the 1960s. At this time architect Peter Locke introduced an ingenious split staircase to help visitors reach the attic from the north wing, which required a stretch of new balustrade on the first floor. When the south staircase – by which visitors now leave the attics – became part of the private accommodation of the tenant/custodians in the 1960s, these attics would otherwise have only accessible by a steep ladder.

These 'quaint garrets', as Morris called them, were likely to have been originally occupied by domestic servants or possibly those working in both house and farm. A Frederick H. Evans photograph of 1896 shows whitewashed struts and a prop supporting the ancient roof of the North Attic. The two garret rooms on the north-east end of the 1660s addition are today furnished with simple painted furniture designed by Ford Madox Brown (and the beds possibly by Philip Webb).

There is clear physical evidence that the gables in the South Attics were raised and ornamented in the late seventeenth century; there is also a surviving pair of simple, elmwood internal shutters. The steep, old south staircase is of a handsome newel construction, and it leads down to the service end of the house.

Left: One of the servants' 'little chambers' in the attics.

Top: The 1960s split staircase rises into this attic.

Middle: The artisan furniture was designed by Ford Madox Brown - and the beds possibly by Philip Webb.

Bottom: The simple staircase leads up to one of the small garret bedrooms.

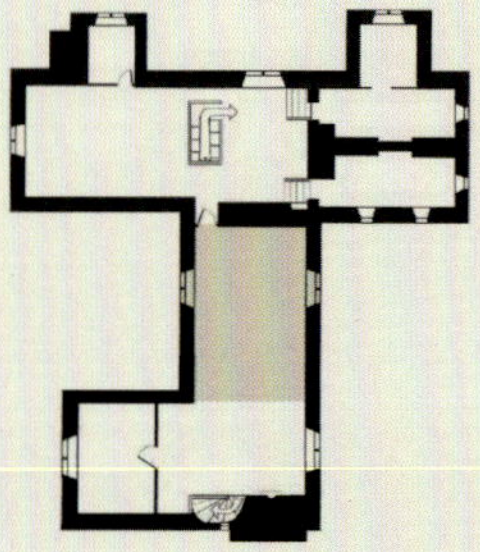

THE EXHIBITION GALLERY (THE MARIGOLD ROOM AND CLOSET)

In the 1611 inventory the 'Chamber over the hall' was mentioned, which, in the eighteenth century, was divided into two and served as part of the tenant's accommodation in the later twentieth century. The larger room, called the Marigold Room after a Morris & Co. wallpaper, and the smaller room or closet, are now used for changing exhibitions. The Cheese Room on the south-west corner - over the former scullery - is used as a study space with accessible reference material, while Jenny Morris's former bedroom - to the east, and over part of the Old Kitchen - is used as an archive and store.

Above: (Detail) Marie Spartali Spilman, *Feeding the Doves*, shows two maids in the service yard.

Opposite left: The Old Kitchen.

Opposite centre: A well-situated privy.

Opposite right: The ample brewhouse.

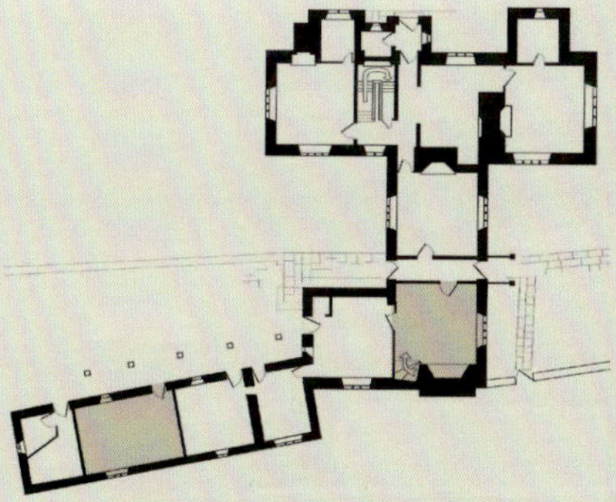

THE OLD KITCHEN AND THE OUTBUILDINGS

At the south end of the original house is the Old Kitchen with its wide hearth. This simply presented, whitewashed room, is part-enclosed on the north side by the elm screen, which creates the screens passage that connects to the hall. On the south wall is the door to the servants' staircase, while to the west is a door that leads to other service rooms around a paved yard.

This part of Kelmscott Manor is principally the realm associated with the practical workings of the household, and the arena of domestic servants on whose shoulders the care of house and family fell. The Morrises employed two generations of a local family called Comely - Mr Comely was the gardener-caretaker and Mrs Comely the cook-housekeeper - and would usually bring other servants up with them from London. They later employed Mr and Mrs Giles as the resident staff (see p.69).

A later low, stone wing – probably seventeenth or early eighteenth century in date and linked to the main house in the nineteenth century – has a pitched roof that forms a covered walkway to the former scullery, laundry and dairy (the latter is now offices). The walkway also leads to the ample brewhouse for the 'wet work' of the household. This has a small hearth and bread oven, and large and small coppers, the first probably for brewing, the other for washing laundry. Outside, the small building with a pyramidal stone roof is a well-situated privy; this served as the principal latrine for the house until the 1920s.

Very unusually for a middle-class Victorian man, Morris, knew his kitchen and brew-house well; a friend recorded, that he was 'a first-rate cook . . .who used to say half-jestingly that he could bake bread and brew ale with any farmer's wife in Oxfordshire'.

SERVANTS' LIVES AT KELMSCOTT MANOR

Until the mid twentieth century, the management of houses such as Kelmscott Manor was predicated on a number of domestic servants. In most upper- and middle-class country residences, servants would travel between the town and country residence, with a caretaker or married couple managing the empty house in the family's absence.

In the summer of 1871, a children's nurse was in attendance on Jane Morris and the children, while Rossetti brought two maidservants from London. The Comelys – Philip and Harriet - acted as caretakers and lived in Garden Cottage - gardener-handyman Philip's habit of touching his hat in deference tending to embarrass the egalitarian-spirited Morris. Harriet Comely was housekeeper (and cook) and was still in post in 1881, when a widow, and remained housed by the Morrises after her retirement. Their niece, Annie, was the only local girl known to have to modelled for Rossetti in the early 1870s, which she did dressed in a housemaid's uniform arranging flowers in the Green Room (see illus p.71).

In 1879, Rossetti mentioned a sixteen-year old maidservant in a letter to Jane Morris, presumably aware that Jane may also have spent time in service in her teenage years. He said his new maid had been in service since she was eleven and 'is quite clever and capable. She will be 17 in September. It is difficult to think of such a kid as being only a year younger than your stately self when I first met you'.

In 1892, William and Mary Giles took over as caretaker-gardener and cook-housekeeper, and their daughter Ada worked as a housemaid. Morris admired Mr Giles's knowledge of plants, and his wife's cooking, writing to Jenny, 'My dinner was served in style, I felt quite proud of such attentions; and Mrs Giles seems a nice kind simple person'. In 1901, William and Emily Panting had taken over from the Gileses, but were dismissed in 1903, and a new gardener Mr Sutton was in post by 1904.

Mr Giles had received a gift of Morris's old top coat and this was given back to Kelmscott Manor by his granddaughter. Caretakers were occasionally

(Detail) Marie Spartali Spilman, *Feeding the Doves*, shows the activity of the service yard at the back of the house.

despatched to pick up visitors from Lechlade station; Morris wrote to Sydney Cockerell, in 1892, 'my trap and man will meet you – waggonette, brown horse, pepper and salt man, NOT in livery'.

Most servants' words are lost to us, but Floss Gunner, who went into service with the Morrises in 1891, was interviewed by *Isis* magazine, in 1965. She said of working as a kitchen-maid in London: 'I used to have to get up about 5 o'clock in the morning, clean the flues, wash up, you know, do all the drudgery'. She recalled washing brass dishes after a party, before her usual five o'clock start.

Floss preferred her time at the country house, saying: 'It was nice to breathe there… It wasn't quite such a drudgery at Kelmscott Manor. It was also very different – I've only got the nicest memories of it.' She remembered Jane with affection, but said of Morris: 'His head was always so much buried in his work that I don't think he'd notice a little thing like me.' But Morris did mention servants in letters to his daughters; in 1887, he writes of a housemaid marrying and being given a silk dress.

In the 1890s, when the family was in residence, Kelmscott Manor's household included a cook, kitchen-maid, house boy, parlourmaid, housemaid, and one 'between the two' – usually known as a 'tweeny'. Floss Gunner would have worked alongside Mary Harding as cook, and her caretaker-gardener husband Francis, as well as general servant Mary Ashley.

As a child, May Morris had also enjoyed the larger domestic household of her paternal grandmother because: 'The family servants were also our playmates in leisure moments. They were of the old school, of course, affectionate, upright and intelligent "knowing their place".' The butler told her that the young William Morris and his friend Burne-Jones were so amusing at the dining table that he had to dash from the room to burst out laughing, as he couldn't be seen laughing by Morris's mother.

Photographs of maids at Kelmscott Manor during May Morris's later years there capture an easier regime. Hilda James, a housemaid from 1922, recalled of May, 'she wasn't proud. You felt at home with her'. After all, Mary Lobb had arrived, in effect, as a gardener-cum-groom before becoming May's devoted friend and companion.

Marigolds, Rossetti, 1874, (detail) for which Annie Comely modelled, housemaid and niece of the Comelys - cook and gardener-handyman at Kelmscott Manor. This painting is in the Nottingham City Museums & Galleries collection.

Maids at Kelmscott captured in a sketch by Hanslip Fletcher of the rear of the Manor, made in 1899.

MORRIS'S *IF I CAN* EMBROIDERY

Worked and designed by Morris in 1857/8 when he lived at 17 Red Lion Square, London, this draws on an interest in textiles that may have been influenced by Morris's travels to the Low Countries when working for architect G. E. Street. Like the *Daisy* hanging, the design of birds and fruit trees was drawn from scenes in Froissart's *Chronicles*. For his first foray into embroidery, Morris tried to replicate the effect of a woven tapestry; he had the material coloured by a French dyer and was assisted by Mary Nicholson, the housekeeper at Red Lion Square, London. One of the very few pieces of embroidery worked by Morris himself, it also hung in Red House and was listed by May Morris in her 1926 memorandum as among the contents to remain at Kelmscott Manor.

MORRIS'S BRASS RUBBINGS FROM GREAT COXWELL CHURCH

This brass bears the inscription: 'Willm Morys, su[m]tyme fermer of cokyswell' and of 'Johane the wyf of Willm Morys'. May Morris recalled: 'One time when my father and mother were taking some friends to see the famous barn at Great Coxwell they went over the church, and they made the rather startling discovery of a handsome late fifteenth century brass of a man and his wife [called William and Jane Morris]... Father took a rubbing of the brass later, and there it is, framed and hanging in one of the lobbies of Kelmscott – rather a ghostly sort of thing to meet one's own epitaph out walking'. Consigned to the attic by the 1960s, the rubbing has been returned to where it hung between 1895 and 1921. The original brasses - 1509 in the case of the husband, the wife undated but similar - are still to be seen in the church at Great Coxwell.

THE BLUE SILK DRESS, ROSSETTI

One of the finest of Rossetti's portraits of Jane Morris who, although by no means his only model, was perhaps his most important muse, inspiring many of his best paintings and drawings. This picture was being worked on in the summer of 1868 and was followed by a series of portraits and portrait sketches painted at Kelmscott Manor. Rossetti composed a Latin verse inscription for the portrait, which may be associated with his c. 1869 sonnet 'The Portrait' which connects the idealisation of love with the making of art.

THE *CABBAGE AND VINE* TAPESTRY

Properly titled *Acanthus and Vine*, this was Morris's first attempt at tapestry weaving. Writing on textiles in *Arts and Crafts Essays* (1893) Morris stated: 'The noblest of the weaving arts is Tapestry, in which there is nothing mechanical: it may be looked upon as a mosaic of pieces of colour made up of dyed threads'. In May 1879, a loom was set up in his bedroom at Kelmscott House in London, and biographer Mackail describes how Morris was 'often up and at work at his loom with the first daylight in spring and summer mornings.' Morris kept a diary, and recorded that between May 10 and September 17, 1879, his weaving occupied 516 hours and thirty minutes. Octavia Hill visited Morris at Kelmscott House in June 1881 and noted: 'He took us all over the garden and into his study . . . The tapestry he had been making himself in his own study was beautiful!!'.

BEDCOVER DESIGNED BY MAY MORRIS

With the individuality of May Morris's design approach, these stylised flora and fauna could all have been seen around the village and in the Manor's own gardens - and clearly reflect the inspiration she found here. Flowers include roses, daisies, ragged robin, irises, poppies and a clump of violets. The top has lines from William Morris's poem 'A Garden by the Sea', and wavy blue lines at the bottom represent the River Thames, with a heron holding an eel in its beak. On the bottom left is an embroidered picture of Kelmscott Manor and St. George's Church; to the right, the Morris motto 'Si Je Puis' and 'Jane Morris', who carried out the embroidery, in around 1910. The side borders are embroidered with butterflies and moths, a ladybird, dragonfly, caterpillar, fish, frog, and birds, including kingfisher, robin, owl and peewit – all then resident around Kelmscott Manor.

PEACOCK INCENSE BURNERS FROM ISFAHAN, IRAN

These were made in the 1870s during the Qajar period in Isfahan, a famous centre for brassworking. The burners are engraved with foliage, figures, animals, and winged creatures pierced in patterns and ornamented with turquoise stones, many now lost. The peacocks' bodies open so that incense can be placed inside and lit. In the 1870s, there was a growing interest in Persian artefacts, and Morris was passionately interested in Middle Eastern art, and was indeed an acknowledged expert on carpets and metalwork on which he advised the South Kensington (now the Victoria & Albert) Museum. The museum's 1876 catalogue has a picture of a similar burner to this pair.

GARRET BEDROOM FURNITURE, FORD MADOX BROWN AND PHILIP WEBB (AND POSSIBLY PHILIP WEBB)

Simple and sturdy, joiner-made using mortise and tenon joints and halved joints with some chamfered edges, these would be described as artisan or craft furniture. They use wood known as 'deal' (softwood pine or fir) and were originally stained - now painted - green. The evidence of May's 1926 memorandum, and the William Morris Centenary exhibition, suggests the beds were probably designed by Webb and all the other items by Ford Madox Brown – the latter once said that what was good enough for the artisan was good enough for his own use. A founding partner of the Firm, Brown supplied more than 300 designs between 1861 and 1875, around 150 for stained glass, the rest for furniture and household items.

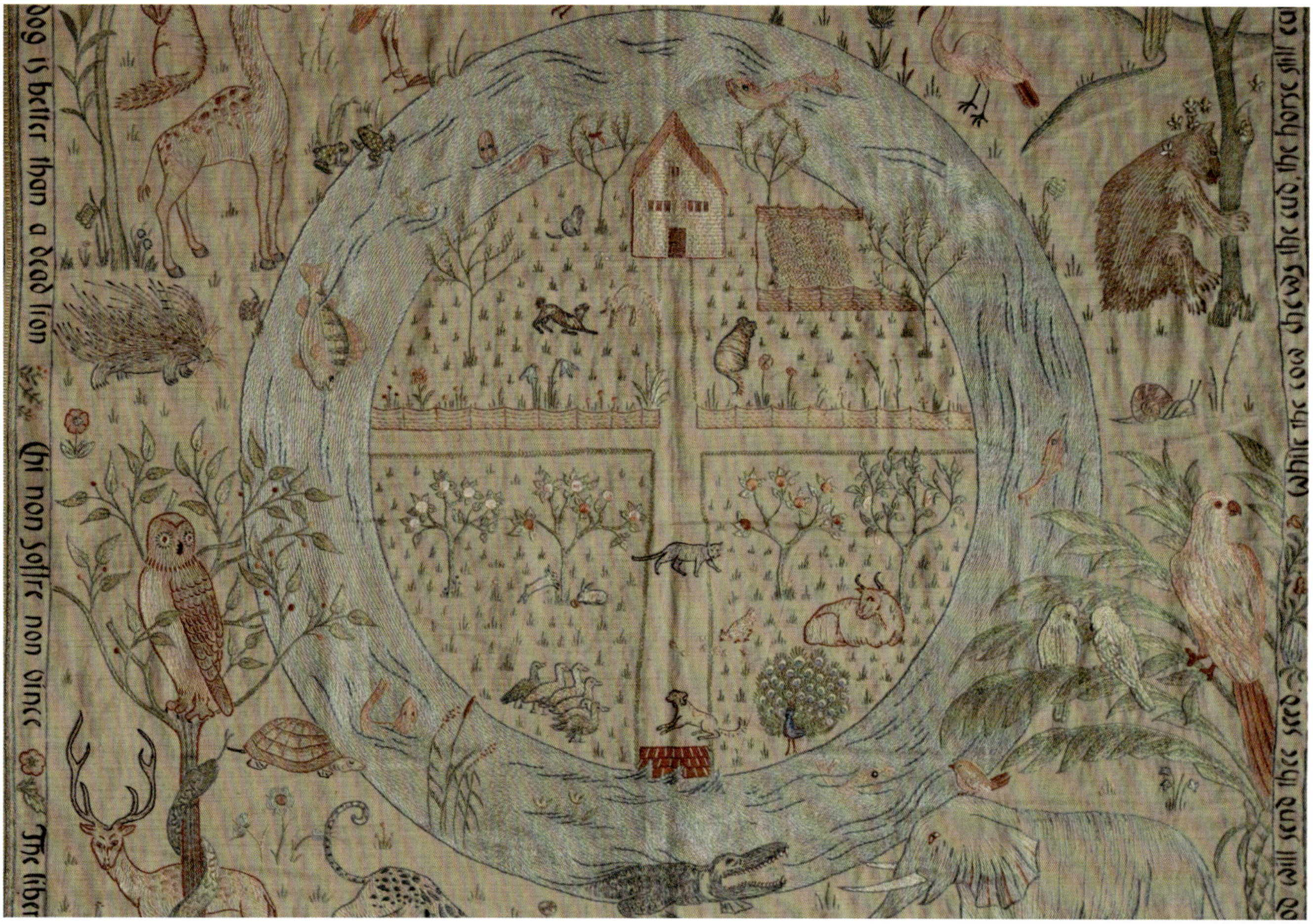

'THE HOMESTEAD AND THE FOREST' QUILT

Designed by May Morris, this cot quilt was embroidered in silk by Jane, in a careful transcription of her daughter's drawing style. At its centre is a depiction of Kelmscott Manor with gardens, an orchard and animals – some clearly drawn from books in Morris's own library. Along the border, quotations and proverbs echo May's enduring socialist values. One of eight pieces exhibited by May at the Arts & Crafts Exhibition Society's third show (1890), it was singled out for praise by *The Illustrated London News*. It has special significance because it dates from the time of May's engagement, and she may later have had a still-born baby. Elfrida Manning, daughter of sculptor Hamo Thorneycroft, visited Kelmscott Manor in March 1925 and noted: 'Miss Morris showed us some coverlets… A charming one for a child, with a little house, a river and every kind of animal - foxes, ducks, a smiling lion and a weak-kneed elephant'. The quilt was bought by May Hobbs (daughter in law of Robert W. Hobbs) of Bradshaw Farm in the 1939 auction of contents. It was from her family that Kelmscott Manor had been bought in 1913. May Hobbs, a professional musician, was also a friend and ally of May so its recent return to the house celebrates a longstanding local farming connection.

THE PRESERVATION AND PRESENTATION OF KELMSCOTT MANOR

Kelmscott Manor is now preserved as a special kind of 'house museum' with authentic contents that communicate a remarkable history. It is a layered story, of which William Morris's occupation is only one chapter. It begins deep in the working landscape, and the house was for most of its history a stone-built working farmhouse and home for the Turner family certainly from the seventeenth century onwards.

For a long time, the Turners' main family residence was Hall Place in Nether Filkins, so Kelmscott Manor was not always at the centre of a single working estate. The house was even divided, and the service end leased for much of the eighteenth century, but the halves reunited in the early nineteenth century for farmer and churchwarden, Charles Turner, and his wife Martha.

When James Turner died in 1869, the farm was a six-hundred-acre estate, and from May 1871, the house and some land were leased as the country home of William and Jane Morris, who shared it with Rossetti until 1874. Indeed, Morris never owned Kelmscott, but leased it first from Charles Hobbs, nephew of James, the land being farmed by Charles's son Robert W. Hobbs (d. 1920) at Home Farm. Robert was an energetic stock breeder and 'gentleman-farmer' who extended the estate to over 2000 acres.

Jane Morris's trustees acquired, on her behalf, Kelmscott Manor and land in the village from Robert Hobbs in 1913. May Morris then inherited the house in 1914 and, resolving that it should be kept as a memorial to her remarkable father, bequeathed it with additional property and important contents

Kelmscott Manor, North West Corner.

to the University of Oxford in 1938. May's will stipulated 'no modern innovations, improvement or installations [are to] be put in or made to the House in the view of its age and its historical interest as the Home of William Morris as it is in the same condition as when he left it'. This was a burdensome condition given the rapidly changing expectations for twentieth-century domestic life and comforts.

Nonetheless, the house was tenanted until 1962, when the University felt unable to keep up with repairs and it passed to the residuary legatee, the Society of Antiquaries of London, which was founded in 1707, and charged by its 1751 Royal Charter with 'the encouragement, advancement and furtherance of the study and knowledge of the antiquities and history of this and other countries'. Morris had been elected a Fellow of the Society in 1894.

John Maddison, FSA and Merlin Waterson, FSA co-authors of the Manor's 2013 Conservation Management Plan (revised in 2018), wrote that Morris was for the Society: 'a figure of symbolic power and relevance' who played a 'decisive role in the transformation of our artistic and political life, and in the protection of our natural and built environment'. Today, the Society preserves Kelmscott Manor in homage to Morris, as a place of resort, reflection, and encounter for anyone to enjoy with scholars regularly revisiting the landscape, architecture, and collections.

Kelmscott Manor from the south-east (left) and within the attic space (right) photographed during the major 1960s programme of repair.

Architects Donald Insall Associates were appointed to carry out extensive repair and conservation works, principally under senior associate Peter Locke. These works of 1964-67, included alterations to help the building function for tenants who kept the principal rooms open to the public, the restrictions on modernising the domestic arrangements having been lifted by a court order. Fortunately, historic farm buildings south of the house were purchased and united with the house in 1967. Kelmscott Manor's public opening began modestly, but annual visitor numbers rose to over twenty thousand by 2018. This required improvements to preserve the manor and gardens, and to protect both the tranquillity of the village and the peaceful encounter with nature that is integral to Kelmscott Manor's reputation.

The 2019-2022 works have been supported by the National Lottery Heritage Fund and other donors, supporting the 'Kelmscott and Morris: Past, Present and Future' Campaign run by the Society of Antiquaries. House and farm buildings have been carefully repaired, by specialist builders Ken Biggs Contractors Ltd of Bristol, and a new single-storey wood-and-thatch structure designed by Architecton serves as a studio and learning space. Following the principles that Webb and Morris helped set out in the manifesto for SPAB, this building - on the axis of a lost cow byre (see p.43) - cannot be mistaken for a historic

View from the barn roof during recent repair works.

barn, but speaks of its day and age while helping families and children to enjoy visiting and learning. The use of thatch, is derived both from records of the original byre and the decision to use it on the new build, is inspired by Morris's love of thatch as a material and his anxiety about it disappearing from Kelmscott's farms in his own time.

In the early years of the Morrises' occupation, furnishing was sparse, like the house in *News from Nowhere* with 'but little furniture, and that only the most necessary, and of the simplest forms'. While the simplicity of the early interiors had a special appeal, the house filled up with furnishings and artworks after Morris's death and during the occupation of Jane as a widow and then of May, and many of the pieces we see today previously furnished Red House, 26 Queen Square or Kelmscott House, as well as May's home at 8 Hammersmith Terrace.

May made a list of the contents in 1926 to be appended to her will, listing those things that would remain with the house. Several of the more important items were left to art galleries and libraries, including Morris's painting of Jane as *La Belle Iseult*, 1858, and the *Prioress's Tale Wardrobe*, 1859 (now at Tate Britain and the Ashmolean, respectively). Many other things, especially ordinary household items, were sadly sold from the house in 1939, after the death of May's companion Mary Lobb. However, what remains is extensive and illuminating: as John Maddison writes, 'a rich and significant record of Morris's life

At work on the relaying of a barn roof at Kelmscott Manor.

Thatching of the new 'learning barn'.

and achievement' – and also of the lives of Jane, May and Jenny and the friends and creative colleagues who passed through these rooms. It should also be seen in the context of other houses which can be visited such as Red House, Bexleyheath, owned by the National Trust, and the William Morris Gallery in Walthamstow.

In a house so long occupied, there are no entirely unaltered rooms, and we cannot 'step back in time'. However, a conscious effort has been made to recover their character and arrangement in the time of the Morris family's occupation – though not at one fixed point of time. Photographs, paintings, and written sources provide evidence of the house Morris loved, and alongside his story are those of Jane, Jenny and May.

There is also the story of the Turners before them, the Hobbses who were their landlords, neighbours, and friends, and indeed the tenants who came after. These include artists Edward Scott-Snell (later Godwin) and his wife Stephani, in the 1940s; and historic buildings expert A. R. 'Dick' Dufty FSA, resident in the 1960s and 70s. The staff, curators, caretakers, Fellows of the Society of Antiquaries of London, and volunteers who have cared for the building, the collections, and the grounds, are also part of the story, as are its many visitors, who each bring their own visions, dreams and questions to this remarkable place.

The completed new 'learning barn' for education, built on the axis of a lost cow byre (see illus p.43).

KELMSCOTT IN ITS WIDER CONTEXT

'Kelmscott lies on the plain of the Thames Valley, but the ground rises up from it gradually, with little interruption of the rise, till the crest of the ridge is gained which lies between Oxfordshire and Worcestershire...

'Gossip about an Old House on the Upper Thames', 1896

Morris had a deep love of landscapes and nature, and would also search local field forms for evidence of the way agriculture changed. He was interested in the history of open field cultivation and its associated common pasture. Later farming was mostly stock-breeding and management, and the cultivation of root crops for fodder. It was dominated by a few families; principally the Turners, with the Edmondses at Manor Farm; the Bradshaws were another leading yeoman family. Charles Hobbs, from whom the Morrises leased Kelmscott Manor, was a nephew of James Turner, who died in 1869. Morris got on well with his son Robert W. Hobbs who farmed the land and who had a 'common interest and common understanding' with Morris.

Morris was also a keen fisherman, rising early with visiting friends to fish for 'pike and perch, dace, chub' – he shared this interest with co-tenant and publisher, F. S. Ellis, who shared the lease at Kelmscott with the Morrises from 1874 to 1884. In a letter to Jenny Morris, in 1888, Morris gave a painterly account of the wildflowers on a local riverbank, noting that: 'the long purples and willow-herb, and that strong-coloured yellow flower very close and very buttony are the great show: but there is a very dark blue-flower, I think mug-wort, mixed with all that besides the purple blossom of the horse-mint and the mouse-ear here and there a bit of meadow-sweet belated'.

Jane Morris also loved the landscape, with perhaps a closer connection through her family from villages around Oxford - Alvescot and Stanton Harcourt. In 1871, she called the area 'delightful and home-like to me, and I love it... every field is lovely by itself, and every house'. In a 1918 letter to Emery Walker, May Morris wrote about her own delight in the woods: 'Such a lovely day, all the shadows very blue and jewel-like, and the green, very green'.

A view from the north west, of St George's, Kelmscott, by Frederick H. Evans in 1896.

A view from the south east today.

Kelmscott was an Anglo-Saxon settlement, the name derived from 'Coenhelm's cott' - the first part probably the name of an Anglo-Saxon landowner, *cott* meaning either a cottage or a smaller settlement associated with a bigger estate. It was then part of the larger manor of Broadwell, owned by Aelfgar, the earl of Mercia, before the Conquest, and retained for its pasture and rich riverside meadows: the river essential for irrigation and carriage, and floodplains providing rich summer grazing.

The cottages of the village clustered around the medieval St George's Church, which was set in open fields and common land, before 'enclosure' in 1799. This effectively redrew the landscape in an attempt to rationalise farming by replacing the rights to cultivate strips in open fields and to pasture animals on the commons. In place of this, enclosure created ownership of compact blocks of hedged fields, to the benefit of the leading landowners over the smallholders who lost their historic rights. In the nineteenth century, most of the villagers of Kelmscott were 'landless' agricultural labourers.

Morris was highly sensitive to the lives of its working people as well as to the simplest vernacular buildings, which dated from a time when, as he wrote in 1877, 'there was a full sympathy between the works of man, and the land they were made for'. In 1889, he wrote of the Kelmscott village houses 'The cottage gardens are bright with flowers; and the cottages themselves mostly models of architecture'.

After Morris's death, Jane commissioned, as a memorial, a pair of cottages (Memorial Cottages) to provide accommodation for farm labourers. These handsome, simple buildings, designed by Philip Webb, include a relief of Morris seated in the 'home mead', carved by George Jack. Completed in 1902, they provide an interesting contrast to the vernacular Garden Cottage by the Manor, originally a pair of seventeenth-century cottages. Another pair of cottages (Manor Cottages) was designed by Ernest Gimson in 1914, at the instigation of May Morris as a memorial to her mother Jane. Gimson also introduced stone-slab sheep fences, following local precedent. These are on a lane that continues past the Plough Inn, and on towards the church.

The William Morris Memorial Hall, Kelmscott, designed by Ernest Gimson in 1914, but only completed by Norman Jewson in 1938.

Memorial Cottages, designed by Philip Webb and completed 1902.

Gimson also designed the village's Morris Memorial Hall in 1914; this was executed by the architect Norman Jewson after Gimson's death - in 1919 - and completed in 1934; built on land donated by Lord Faringdon, with stone donated by Stafford Cripps from his adjoining Filkins estate. It opened in 1934, on the centenary of Morris's birth, after May had doggedly raised money for nearly fifteen years, asking all Manor visitors to donate. After the Memorial Hall the lane turns past the 1898 former village school, which May supported in various ways. Opposite this lies the parish church of St George's. The nave is of two principal periods of construction in the twelfth century, while its chancel is early thirteenth-century. The transepts are later thirteenth century, and there are later fourteenth- and fifteenth-century alterations – in all just the layered effect Morris especially valued.

Morris wrote of it in 1895: 'The church . . is small but interesting; the mass of it, a nave with a tiny aisle, transept, and chancel, being Early English of date, though the arches of the aisle are round-headed . . . Most of the windows (which are insertions of the early 14th century) have their inner arches elegantly cusped . . . A very beautiful bell-cot formed by two trefoil arches crowns the eastern gable of the nave and composes pleasantly with the low-pitched roofs over a clerestory'. He savoured the details of its historic evolution, writing: 'The church is plastered almost all over the walls, as no doubt it was in the earliest days: it is fortunate in having escaped the process of stripping and pointing which so many of our village churches have undergone at the hands of the restoring wise-acres'. There are also some very fine thirteenth-century wall paintings in a strong red ochre.

St George's also contains monuments of the Turner family who occupied Kelmscott Manor for many generations. In a southeast corner of the churchyard, close to the church, is the simple monument to William and Jane Morris, designed by Webb and carved by Lawrence Turner. Webb wrote to Jane in 1897: describing it as 'a semblance of a roof . . . I have made it rudely simple, dividing the slope into the required four spaces'. Here too are buried Jenny and May.

A detail of the wallpaintings in Kelmscott Church.

The Morris family's gravestone, designed by Philip Webb.

BIBLIOGRAPHY AND ACKNOWLEDGEMENTS

This text is indebted to previous guidebooks by A. R. 'Dick' Dufty, *Kelmscott: An illustrated Guide*, 1996; John Cherry, *Kelmscott Manor: An Illustrated Guide*, 2004, and Christopher Catling, *Kelmscott Manor*, 2011. The recent John Maddison and Merlin Waterson, *Kelmscott Manor Conservation Management Plan*, 2013 (revised 2018), has been of particular help, as has detailed architectural analysis by Nicholas Cooper and the recent archaeological report by Wessex Archaeology. Other essays and articles and advice from John Maddison, Peter Cormack, Paul Drury, Tessa Wild and Nicholas Cooper have proved very useful, as has advice from Tim Richardson on the garden's influence. Both Gavin Williams, property manager, and Kathy Haslam, curator, have been extremely generous with time, guidance, and advice, as well access to valuable new research by Kelmscott Manor's own dedicated team of volunteer researchers.

For the history, archaeology and an assessment of the landscape, vernacular architecture, and social and economic history of the village of Kelmscott as well as the Manor, Alan Crossley, Tom Hassall, Peter Salway, (eds), *William Morris's Kelmscott: Landscape and History*, Windgather Press, 2007, is recommended; which includes an enlightening assessment of alterations since Morris's time in 'Kelmscott Manor as William Morris Never Knew It', by Jonathan Howard. Helen Wyld reported on the tapestries in 2013 and Patrick Baty produced a paint analysis report in February 2021.

On William and Jane Morris, Fiona MacCarthy, *William Morris: A Life for our Time*, Faber and Faber, 1995, *The Routledge Companion to William Morris*, Routledge, 2021, and Jan Marsh's, *Jane & May Morris: a biographical story, 1839-1938*, The Printed Word, 2000, are recommended, as are editions of the letters of William Morris's (edited by N. Kelvin) and Jane Morris (ed. J. Marsh and F. C. Sharp). For Jane, also see Wendy Parkins, *Jane Morris: The Burden of History*, 2013. For Rossetti, see William E.Fredeman, ed, *The Correspondence of Dante Gabriel Rossetti*, Boydell and Brewer, 2002 (and ongoing); and Jan Marsh, *Dante Gabriel Rossetti: Painter & Poet*, Orion, 2005, and Julian Treuherz, Elizabeth Prettejohn, Edwin Becker, *Dante Gabriel Rossetti*, the Walker Art Gallery, 2003. For other Morris homes, David Rodgers, *William Morris At Home*, Ebury Press and the William Morris Society, Ebury Press, 1996.

For the artistic influence of Morris, see Linda Parry (ed), *William Morris*, Philip Wilson Publishers & the Victoria and Albert Museum, 1996; Leonard Stoppani (ed), *William Morris & Kelmscott*, Design Council, 1981, Tessa Wild, *William Morris & his Palace of Art*, Philip Wilson Publishers, 2018; for a fuller consideration of the artistic achievement of May Morris, see Anna Mason et al, *May Morris: Arts & Crafts Designer*, V&A Museum, 2017, and Linda Parry (ed), *William Morris: Art and Kelmscott*, Boydell Press & Society of Antiquaries, 1996. The latter includes the memories of A. R. 'Dick' Dufty, the President of the Society of Antiquaries in 1978, who masterminded the 1960s restoration, and was a resident curator-tenant. For the memories and letters of another Kelmscott tenant, see: Joscelyn Godwin (ed), *The Starlight Years: Love & War at Kelmscott Manor 1940-1948*, Dovecote Press, 2015.

Jeremy Musson, FSA
Cambridge 2022

The bedcover on William Morris's bed, designed by May Morris and embroidered by Jane Morris.

Attic at Kelmscott Manor, 1880s, watercolour by May Morris.

Love is enough: though the World be a-waning,
And the woods have no voice but the voice of complaining,
Though the sky be too dark for dim eyes to discover
The gold-cups and daisies fair blooming thereunder,
Though the hills be held shadows, and the sea a dark wonder
And this day draw a veil over all deeds pass'd over,
Yet their hands shall not tremble, their feet shall not falter;
The void shall not weary, the fear shall not alter
These lips and these eyes of the loved and the lover.

From William Morris, 'Love is Enough' 1868

We are especially grateful to the William Morris Gallery for their kind support. Thanks too, to Susannah Stone for her help with picture research and Harriet Salisbury for reading the text for me.

ISBN: 978-0-85431-303-7

Picture Credits, Chris Challis (in 2022) unless otherwise
Robin Forster, 18 (right)
London Metropolitan Archive, 19 (right)
William Morris Gallery, London Borough of Waltham Forest, 18 (left), 19 (left), 22 (right), 30, 32-33, 42 (right), 44-45, 71 (right), 86 (left), 94
Jeremy Musson, 37, 82, 89 (right), 91
National Portrait Gallery, 15, 20, 25, 28, 29
Nottingham City Museums & Galleries / Bridgeman Images, 71 (left)
Chris Poolman/Ken Biggs Construction 86
Society of Antiquaries of London, 6, 9, 21, 22 (left), 27, 34, 35, 36, 37, 39, 40, 41, 42 (left), 43, 64, 65, 68, 72, 73, 74, 75, 76, 77, 78, 79, 80, 81, 82, 84, 85, 87, 88, 90, 92
The Trustees of the British Museum, 17 (right)
Victoria & Albert Museum, London, 16, 19 (left)

Text written by Jeremy Musson, Cambridge
Design by Steve Hayes
Printed by Blackmore Ltd, Shaftesbury